Mrs. Lester's Girls and Their Service, by the Author of 'Miss Marston's Girls and Their Confirmation'

MRS. LESTER'S GIRLS.

"She clutched her umbrella, and turned to meet the furious animal."—*Page* 17.

Frontispiece.

MRS. LESTER'S GIRLS

AND

THEIR SERVICE.

BY THE AUTHOR OF

"MISS MARSTON'S GIRLS AND THEIR CONFIRMATION," &c.

" How blessed, from the bonds of sin
And earthly fetters free,
In singleness of heart and aim,
Thy servant, Lord, to be!
The hardest toil to undertake
With joy at Thy command,
The meanest office to receive
With meekness at Thy hand!

" With willing heart and longing eyes,
To watch before Thy gate,
Ready to run the weary race,
To bear the heavy weight;
No voice of thunder to expect,
But follow calm and still,
For love can easily divine
The One Beloved's will."

SPITTA.

LONDON:

JAMES NISBET & CO., 21 BERNERS STREET.

MDCCCLXXXV.

PREFACE.

THE following stories are intended to illustrate and convey truth to the minds of young women, especially those in domestic service.

There are not a few of these, desirous of doing their duty and open to religious influences, who may not have had the opportunity of being taught the simple truths of the gospel, or at least, may never have seen the importance of being constantly guided by the light of God's Spirit shining through His Word. In the hope of helping such this little book is written.

The characters delineated are types of many to be found in real life; they represent the evil and danger which result from want of sound principle, and the happy effects of Christian principle on the hearts and lives of those who are guided by it.

That blessing from above may rest upon the readers of this little volume is the earnest prayer of one who desires to serve their best interests.

MRS. LESTER'S GIRLS, AND THEIR SERVICE.

In a flower garden we expect to find a variety of plants. There will be the hardy ones, which are able to stand alone in rough winds and scorching heat ; perhaps also, the clinging, climbing plants, which need to lean upon what is stronger than themselves. There too, perchance, we may find the delicate flowers, which must be sheltered, and whose fine qualities call for all the skill and care of the gardener to develop them. Some plants may require exposure to the sun, whilst others must be kept in the shade. North winds, and cold, and storm have all their work to do, as well as south winds, sunshine, and refreshing showers.

Mrs. Lester's Bible-class, like the enclosure of a garden, had in it a variety of characters, and it is of some of these I am about to write.

MRS. LESTER'S GIRLS

AND THEIR SERVICE.

———◆———

CHAPTER I.

"Dare to be true: nothing can need a lie;
A fault which needs it most grows two thereby."
— G. HERBERT.

IN the kitchen of a country cottage sat a young girl crying bitterly. Her mother, a weary sufferer, had but an hour before sunk to rest in the sleep which knows no waking till the resurrection morn.

The girl's father and brother, who had been working at a little distance from their home, were sent for when poor Mrs. Carter's end seemed drawing near, so that they and her only daughter Matilda, beside two kind-hearted neighbours, were with her when she passed away. She was a good woman, and had long been looking forward to her great change.

The painful parting over, the last gentle sigh

A

breathed, Mrs. Robson and her daughter persuaded the weeping family to leave the room. After giving way to their grief for a time, the father and his son went out to make some arrangements. Matilda took a low seat in one of the wide chimney corners, and, left to herself, a sense of utter loneliness and helpless distress completely overcame her.

She thought over her mother's words—never to be forgotten—"You'll be a good girl to your father, Mattie; won't you, dear? My poor child! May God Almighty take care of you! Don't fret for me. I'm going home;—going to be with my blessed Saviour."

"How can I help fretting?" Mattie said to herself, as she sobbed convulsively. "I shall miss mother so much, oh! so very much! Whatever shall I do without her? She's been such a good mother to me. It's terrible lonesome! Poor mother! Oh dear! oh dear!"

After a time the clergyman's wife looked in. She soothed and cheered poor Mattie, and prayed with her before leaving. Presently Mrs. Benson sent a young servant to sit with her.

Next morning an aunt came to stay a few days with Mattie, to help her in making the necessary preparations before the sad day of the funeral. Time wore on slowly and heavily with the sorrowful child, though there was plenty of work to be done.

Her two brothers, who lived some miles away, came to follow their mother to the grave with the rest of the family and many other relations. Mattie's aunt stayed on to help her to put things straight after Mrs. Carter's death, and was then obliged to leave her niece to do the best she could to keep house for her father and brother.

Matilda was only twelve years old, but her mother had taught her to be useful. For a girl of her age, Mattie could do plain needlework and mending very well; what little cooking was needed had been done by her for some time past, and she was not altogether unaccustomed to the use of brooms and brushes. She had been kept from school by her mother's illness, but went back to it a few days after the funeral. Her spirits gradually returned, though she missed her mother sadly in the house. Being naturally high-spirited, and sometimes rather boisterous and rough, her liveliness often led her into mischief; Mattie had faults and failings, but she had also many good points in her character.

One of the most excellent qualities shone brightly in her, and that was *truthfulness*. Her mother had taught her early the importance of being truthful both in words and actions, and always set a good example of this herself. Everybody knew that Jane Carter's word might be depended upon, as she never asserted anything to· be true without being sure of it. If she was aware that the eager Matilda was making too much of whatever she might be relating, Mrs. Carter would require the child to stop and recall her words, pointing out the exaggeration. Should Mattie be reproved and endeavour to make her fault appear less than it really was, her mother took pains to show her that such conduct was wrong. The child learnt to love and admire truthfulness, and to hate and despise falsehood and deceit as mean and cowardly. She was a courageous girl, and as soon as she was able to understand the evil of deception would never lower herself by saying or acting what was untrue. You could see at a glance that Mattie might be trusted to speak the truth, she appeared so honest and straightforward, and able to look you well in the face as having nothing to hide; yet was she neither bold nor given to vulgar staring.

The poor child was left very much to herself after her mother's death; but her father was kind and affectionate, and, when he came home of an evening, he endeavoured to interest himself with what his young daughter had learnt at school. Mattie tried to be friendly only with such girls as her mother would have approved. Her liveliness, however, made her a general favourite, and no girlish game seemed to go well without her.

According to custom, one bright summer day

the parish school treat took place in the Rectory garden and paddock adjoining. There was swinging; races were run for toys, and scrambles were given; the girls played at " drop-handkerchief" and similar games, whilst the boys enjoyed their cricketing; and all the usual amusements at such times were entered into with spirit by the children, and by the kind teachers and friends who had come to help them.

Then the happy party assembled to have tea on the Rectory lawn, and, judging by the rapid disappearance of plum-cake and other provisions, they enjoyed and did justice to the feast. After this, Mr. Benson, the clergyman, gave an address, which was followed by a short prayer and the singing of a hymn; then the prizes were distributed, and the children dispersed to have a few more games before returning home.

Mattie was in wild spirits. She and some of her companions took to playing at bat-and-trap. They had been warned several times not to go near the house, but were too excited to give much heed to the warning.

" I mean to have ten this time," exclaimed Mattie, as she struck the ball with force.

There was a crash. The girls stood still and held their breath in dismay; and then one or two of them rushed round by the side of the house to conceal themselves. Mattie's first impulse was to do the same, but the next minute she came slowly back, feeling that it was cowardly to run away, and frightened as she was, she yet knew it was only right to confess to having broken the window. Many hastened towards the house to see what harm was done, the Rector amongst the number. There was a dead pause whilst he exclaimed, "Who is it who has broken my drawing-room window?"

Various opinions were expressed. The girls who had been playing near were mentioned. It was not remembered that Mattie had been one of them, and as her companions would deny having done it without exposing her, it might never have been known who broke the window, so *she* thought, but at the same time she came forward trembling, and gasped out, "Please, sir, I did it."

"*You*, Mattie! how was it you were so careless?"

"We were playing at bat-and-trap, sir. I struck the ball hard, and it hit the window."

"You'd no business to play so near the Rectory," said the schoolmaster. "You had been warned against doing so several times."

"I'm very sorry it happened," said Mattie, whose tears began to flow.

"Well, Matilda, I must excuse it. It was an accident. We must not have any tears to-day," said the kind old gentleman. The sight of Mattie's black dress made it impossible for him to say anything harsh to the motherless girl, and severity was not a feature in his character.

"I. hope it will be a lesson to you," said the schoolmaster; "and that in future you will pay more attention to what you're told. When Mr. Benson is so kind as to let you have the treat in his garden, it's really too bad to break his window. It's very vexing!"

"Don't say any more about it," said the Rector. "We must have a different arrangement about the games another time. It is not every girl who would come forward so frankly to confess to having done the mischief. This makes me the more ready to overlook Matilda's carelessness than I should have been, had she attempted to hide the truth."

"Well, sir," said the schoolmaster, "I will say this for Mattie Carter—whatever her faults may be, Mrs. Bell and I have always known her to speak the truth."

"That's right, my child! *Always dare to be true,*" and Mr. Benson patted Mattie's shoulder, whilst she whispered as he walked away, "Oh, sir, I am so sorry."

About two years after his wife's death, Carter married again, and Matilda went to a little place of service. She was rough and careless, which failings often brought her into trouble; but she never made false excuses, neither did she try to excuse herself by speaking of things which had really happened, but were no hindrances to her. Mattie would not attempt to hide the truth by only telling half of it, as is the way with some people. She was really sincere, and always endeavoured to avoid giving a false colouring to what she said. Therefore those she was with learnt to trust her word. She was never suspected of untruthfulness, nor of aiming to deceive, as must ever be the case with people who have proved themselves false.

At fifteen, Mattie left her first place, in hope of finding one where she could learn more of work. It was not long before she heard that Mrs. Turner, of Wilminster, was wanting a nursemaid. It was a tempting situation; Mattie longed to obtain it, but Mrs. Turner made a great point of having a girl at least sixteen years of age. Matilda was tall, and would have passed for older than she was, and some girls as young as she would have made out that they were turned sixteen, but she knew better than to be so untrue.

Truthfulness with Mrs. Turner was an indispensable requisite, and, since Matilda had not deceived her in the first instance, the lady felt rather inclined to take Mattie, as she had a good character, so it was decided for her to go to Mrs. Turner's on trial.

Matilda was, at first, shy and awkward. She needed much teaching, both as to behaviour and as to her duties; but she was willing and desirous to learn, and on the whole a good girl. Occasionally, indeed, she would allow herself to be overcome by a fit of idleness and shirk her work. Now and then Mattie was found fault with for being slovenly or rough, but she was not intentionally naughty, and would try to make amends for her faults by increased diligence and care. She improved as time went on, and became at length a very nice servant.

The nursemaid before her had been dismissed for not only being untruthful herself, but for teaching the innocent children under her charge to be untrue and to deceive their parents, which was more wicked still. Therefore, Mrs. Turner was extremely particular as to whom she took in Caroline's place, and both mistress and nurse watched Matilda carefully till they were satisfied they could trust her.

Mrs. Turner had asked Mrs. Lester to allow Matilda to attend her Bible-class, and when she had become acquainted with some of the girls she began to feel at home and liked it very much. Elsie Dale, of whom I shall presently speak, was a great favourite there, and very kind to Mattie.

One bright autumn day, she and Esther the nurse were dressing the little ones to go out—

"You've got forward with your work, Matilda," said Esther, "and, as it's so pleasant ánd sunny, I think we'll start for Lovelands Wood."

This was a chosen resort with both young and old, and worthy of its name. It was but a mile from Mrs. Turner's house, and, should little feet be tired, there would be time to rest on reaching the place. Roads were cut through the wood in several directions, winding under the shade of large-trunked oaks, beeches, slender birches with silvery stems, firs of various kinds, mountain ashes, with their bright orange or scarlet berries in the autumn, and a variety of other trees and shrubs, whilst occasionally a joyous squirrel might be seen leaping from bough to bough.

In the spring-time, the wood was musical with the sweet songs of the birds, the cooing of the wood-pigeon, and the murmuring, perhaps, of some streamlet over its stony bed.

In the summer, wild hyacinths with their blue bells, mauve foxgloves, rosy ragged-robins, and the sweet-scented woodruff took the place of the primroses, anemones, and dog-violets which had carpeted the ground; whilst the banks of the little streams were gay with forget-me-nots and the golden blossoms of kingcups, and the crystal water rippled

over bright green cresses. The branches of sapling
oaks were festooned with trailing honeysuckle, and
grey lichens hung from the trees in bunches of hairy
threads.

Sometimes the ringing voices of happy children
sounded through the wood, and added life to this
peaceful spot, which was attractive for various
reasons.

In the autumn, blackberries abounded, and the
hazel-bushes were loaded with nuts, and, as Christmas approached, the wood was sought for bunches of
holly and sprays of mistletoe.

The ivy sometimes covered the ground with tiny
leaves. It climbed the trunks of many trees, and
occasionally one was to be seen which it had en-
veloped in a rich green shroud, and had gradually
hugged to death. Graceful ferns and soft mosses,
besides many other pretty things, made their home
in the wood.

Matilda was arriving at that awkward age when
young people often feel inclined to resent being
treated as children, and begin to assume the manners
of those older than themselves, but, not having their
confidence, and not knowing how to behave as if
they were grown up, they are not unfrequently very
shy and uncomfortable and remiss in their behaviour
to their superiors without any intention of being
rude.

She took charge of the two little walkers, and Esther started wheeling the baby in the perambulator. She was slow to trust him to other hands than her own. They had not gone far when Mrs. Lester appeared coming towards them.

"Isn't that lady your Sunday teacher?" said Esther.

"Yes, sure enough, it's Mrs. Lester," replied Matilda.

"Mind you make your curtsey to her."

"Is it my place to do so?" asked Mattie, looking frightened.

"Yes, of course it is. It's for *you* to show respect to your teacher first, and then, I daresay, she'll notice you."

Mrs. Lester met the party, but did not know Mrs. Turner's children; and as Matilda, who was colouring up and wishing herself anywhere else, had turned her face in another direction, it was not to be expected that Mrs. Lester should recognise her. Matilda was, however, somewhat disappointed to think that she had missed a kind word and look from her teacher, and in consequence a little vexed with herself for her behaviour.

"Well, Matilda, I am surprised at you!" was Esther's remark, when the lady had passed them. After a pause the nurse continued, "By-the-bye, I noticed the other day that when your mistress met us you made no curtsey to her, but walked on as if you did not know her. Mind you don't do so again. My mother was very particular with me," Esther added. "She used to say, 'You're bound to show your mistress the respect of curtseying to her just as a soldier has to salute an officer, or as a man-servant is expected to touch his hat to any member of his master's family.' If I, at my age, do not feel it beneath me to make a curtsey, surely *you* need not. We never lower ourselves by treating others with the respect due to them."

"But, nurse, I don't think servants always behave as you say I should."

"Very likely not. If so, probably they are as yourself, young and ignorant; and perhaps, unlike you, they may not have had any one to teach them better manners."

Mattie felt rather annoyed with the nurse's plain speaking, but knew she practised what she taught, and that she was one whom everybody respected. Well was it for the poor motherless girl that she was under such good guidance! By degrees Mattie became so respectful and quiet in her manner as to win general approval, and the deference she learnt readily to show wherever it was due gained for her respect and consideration in return. Presently the nurses changed hands, and Mattie pushed forward the perambulator.

"Nursie, will you pick us some of the flowers by the stream?" said one of the children.

"Yes, but we shall have to walk faster. Be careful with baby," she said to Mattie, "we're going on in front."

Esther looked back more than once, and saw that the girl was proceeding steadily with him. It was not long, however, before Matilda met with an acquaintance of hers. She left the child for some minutes, with his head hanging over the perambulator in the warm autumn sun, whilst she stood talking with her friend. Esther saw this from a little distance, and hastened back, feeling anything but pleased. I need not repeat the conversation that followed, but will only add that Matilda took good care never to do so again.

In one visit to the wood the children were looking for ferns, which Mattie dug up for them with a trowel brought for the purpose. Esther was a little behind with the baby. The sound of cart wheels was heard rapidly approaching, but the cart could not be seen on account of a curve in the road. A party of children were hunting for blackberries. Matilda was the first to catch sight of the horse, which was coming on at a jog-trot. The driver had apparently fallen asleep, or was intoxicated. To her horror, she saw a baby, of perhaps two years old, sitting in the middle of the road, playing with the pebbles.

Shrieking out, " Stop ! the child !" Mattie rushed forward, to the astonishment of Esther, who wondered what was the matter. The girl did not cease running till within a few inches of the horse's feet, when she snatched up the child, placed it in safety, and returned to the children with slow and tottering steps.

"Well done, Matilda !" was Esther's exclamation, in a husky tone, as soon as she had any voice to speak. " You've saved the life of that little one! the mother shall know of this."

Esther would any day have risked her life to save that of a child, and she fully appreciated the effort which Matilda had made, who rose in the nurse's esteem from that day forward.

Whilst Mattie was resting, having turned faint with the excitement, Esther hastened to find the children who had so carelessly let the baby crawl into the road, to tell them to what danger they had exposed it, and to ascertain who was the child's mother, and where she lived. Esther was not long in finding an opportunity of visiting the woman, who was, as might be expected, truly grateful to Mattie, and came to thank her the next day, bringing her a pretty present.

In another visit to the wood, Matilda had charge of two of the children, Esther not being able to accompany them. They had all had a very happy time, gathering moss, and picking up fir cones and other treasures, which were carried home in the baskets they had taken with them. The little girls were eager to make some pretty things like those made by Caroline, the former nursemaid.

On leaving the wood, they came into the long avenue. It was wide enough for a carriage drive. The trees looked enchantingly beautiful overhead. A trunk had been felled, and was lying on the grass. The children hailed it with delight, and all sat down to rest and enjoy themselves.

Soon, however, their attention was arrested by the howling and whining of a dog. Being afraid of dogs, they became anxious to return home as quickly as possible. Looking back, they saw one at a distance come creeping along. Catching sight of them, it commenced running. They were much alarmed, and hurried forward. Once or twice Miss Amy looked behind her, but each time she did so it growled. The poor children screamed with fright.

Matilda was at her wit's end to know what to do. The savage-looking creature was close upon them, and the children were under her charge. She felt the responsibility. The dog was clearing the ground rapidly, but thought could travel faster still. Through the young girl's mind flashed the remembrance of the story of Eric, the Russian servant, giving himself up to the wolves, to save his master and his master's daughter. Matilda's resolution was made. Telling the children not to wait for her, but to take the turn which would now bring them quickly into the high road, and to run as fast as they could, she clutched her umbrella and turned to meet the furious animal, uttering from her heart the prayer, "Lord, save me!" which she felt immediately assured was heard.

Mattie's morning and evening prayers had been regularly repeated for years past, but never till now did she really pray. It was but a very short petition, but in that moment strength and peace were given to her. The ferocious dog was just ready to spring upon her, when a shrill whistle stopped it; another, and the sullen and disappointed creature turned back to obey the call. Now Mattie knew that God had heard her, and that He was *her* God. She at once dropped on her knees to thank Him for His preserving care, and never, from that time, could she forget that the Lord was ever present to hear and answer prayer.

Her fears had perhaps been excessive, but she was young; no one appeared at hand to help, her mistress's children were under her charge, and the anxiety Mattie felt was as much for them as for herself. A bite from a dog, even when not mad, is an alarming thing, and the frightened girl was by no means sure that this was not a case of madness.

The entreaty for deliverance was doubly answered. It was the first cry of faith laying hold of God through

B

Christ. Instantly the answer came, not merely by Mattie's being preserved from personal injury, but also by the assurance conveyed to her heart that she was the Lord's, and in His safe keeping.

The simple truth of the gospel, instilled into her mind from earliest years, but hitherto only received by her natural understanding, was now suddenly brought home with Divine reality and power.

No words could express the change Mattie felt wrought in her, but from this time she rested on Christ as her Saviour, and rejoiced in God as her reconciled Father.

She could not rise from her knees without a few moments' quiet thought and prayer. Then she hastened forward to the terrified children, who clung to her in great excitement. She told them that a man had called off the dog, and how thankful they all ought to be that it had not bitten them.

Arrived at home, the little girls eagerly related the adventure. Their parents rejoiced that they and their young nursemaid had escaped unhurt, and esteemed Mattie much for her courageous conduct.

They learnt afterwards that the dog was an ill-tempered creature, under training, and usually chained up on account of its fierceness. Having just been beaten, it was intent on revenging itself where it could.

Mattie's was one of the comparatively rare cases of conversion in which the words of Isaiah are fulfilled, "I am found of them that sought me not." She had always understood that she was a sinner in need of the Saviour, but had never claimed Him for her own before that moment, when, in answer to her cry for temporal help, the truth darted through her mind, like a flash of lightning, that she belonged to the Lord, who had bought her with His blood, and that He was indeed her Saviour and her God. She had had no long weary night of groping after the "True Light," neither had she the twilight of seeking Christ amidst doubts and fears, but the Sun of Righteousness had risen suddenly upon her, like daybreak in Eastern countries, without any twilight to precede it; and it was the dawn of an everlasting day! Happy for her that she had been taught the way of salvation in early years, and had not to contend with ignorance! and that when the Lord was revealed to her she was made willing to receive Him as a little child!

On the whole, Mattie had always been considered a good girl, but, it need scarcely be said, that from henceforth she was more than ever desirous of fulfilling her duties well, for a stronger motive than before was actuating her—love to the Saviour, who had died to deliver her from hell and bring her to heaven, led her most earnestly to wish to please Him in all things, even in her little common services and everyday employments.

She grew in the knowledge of her own need and sinfulness, and in the desire to know more of Christ, thus learning truly to value the Scriptures and to love prayer. She longed to be useful to other girls who might never have had her advantages, especially that of a Christian mother. At present, however, Mattie did not see her way, but she had not many weeks to wait before an opportunity of usefulness was placed before her.

She often heard allusion made to Caroline by the children or servants, all of whom seemed to have been very fond of her, notwithstanding her sad fault and the disgrace in which she left Mrs. Turner. Mattie gathered that Caroline was pretty and had very pleasing manners, that she was kind-hearted and obliging, and very clever with her fingers. As far as Mattie could make out, the former nursemaid seemed to have been pleasant and nice in every respect, except in one grievous failing,—she was utterly careless about speaking the truth. This, of course, spoilt her whole character, by taking away its very foundation.

Matilda also found that Caroline's mother had died when her daughter was very young; that the girl's father had married again about two years after his first wife's death; and that the stepmother was quite a different person from Caroline's own mother, who had married beneath her, and was gentle and refined; whilst the second Mrs. Hall was a rough and vulgar woman. Having but little sympathy, and not being naturally fond of children, she had brought up her stepdaughter with harshness and severity. The consequence was, that the child fell into very deceitful ways, until it became quite as easy for her to say what was false as what was true. She would as soon do so as not, even when there was no fear of punishment to prompt the lie. Real faults were often unnoticed by this woman, whilst slighter ones were unduly punished when they inconvenienced her. She was, moreover, by no means truthful herself when it suited her purpose to be otherwise. No wonder that Caroline, who was timid by nature, tried to screen herself from punishment by falsehood and deceit! As she grew up, her stepmother became increasingly jealous and suspicious of her, being always ready to think that the girl looked down upon her, and wished to appear superior to herself, because Caroline's own mother had been in a higher position in life. Mrs. Hall could not sympathise with Caroline's refined feelings and tastes, but despised them as affected and unpractical. Edmund Hall knew that his wife and daughter were not on the best terms, but he little guessed how much the latter had to bear. His

second wife could never be to him what his first wife
had been, but she was industrious, clean, and steady,
and she made her husband comfortable. He was
very fond of Caroline, and sorry that there should
ever be any unpleasantness between her and her
stepmother.

Mattie felt quite distressed for the girl on hearing
her history, and thankful that she herself had been
brought up differently, and that she had found a kind
and true friend in her own stepmother.

"What are you crying for, Master Walter?" she
asked one night when she went up to bed.

"O 'Tilda! you have been so long in coming!
I've been thinking every minute that the black man
would come and take me away."

"What black man? What are you talking about?
You must be dreaming, dear."

"Why Caroline told me there was a black man
who came and carried off children, if they'd been
naughty in the day; and it all seemed so dark,"
sobbed the child.

"Caroline was a bad girl to frighten you with such
nonsense. Don't you believe any such thing. Now
go to sleep, there's a dear!"

"Are you very sure there isn't a black man,
'Tilda?"

"Yes, quite sure. It was only a wicked story that
Caroline told. Ask your Mama about it to-morrow."

" Caroline never would let me tell my Mama. If Caroline was naughty, she was very kind too. She gave me my little horse, and my box of bricks. I do love her. Won't she hear about it if I tell my Mama?"

"No, dear; she's gone now. Tell your Mama what you like," and Matilda kissed and soothed the little one to sleep.

We will now leave Mattie for the present, watching for a special opportunity of helping some girl less favoured than herself, but at the same time ready to make use of any lesser occasions for doing good to others.

CHAPTER II.

"Little deeds of kindness,
Little words of love,
Make our earth an Eden
Like the heaven above.

Little seeds of mercy,
Sown by youthful hands,
Grow to bless the nations
Far in heathen lands."

A LITTLE out of Wilminster, on the Westmeade road, stood a pretty cottage covered with creepers. The garden in front, though small, was gay with choice flowers, which were evidently trained and tended by one who understood and valued them. Beehives were ranged along the wall. In the porch stood a young woman of perhaps six-and-twenty, leaning on crutches. She appeared full of pleasant expectation, as she gazed first in one direction then in the other. It was Elsie Dale, who was before mentioned as having been kind to Matilda Carter when she joined the Bible-class.

A girl of thirteen came out of the house and clasped

Elsie's hand in hers, exclaiming, "Auntie, I do wish I belonged to Mrs. Lester's class!"

"You're not old enough, Minnie; I cannot see why you should wish it, for you have a good and kind teacher at the Sunday-school, and you like the girls you are with, and are getting on nicely with your lessons."

"Yes, the girls are all very well, but I love Mattie."

"Oh, that's your reason! Then I'm afraid you'll have to wait two years yet."

Minnie heaved a sigh.

"Well, dear, if we're spared, you and I will go to class together some day."

"All right, Auntie! and now I'm going to look for Mattie," and Minnie bounded to the gate. The four visitors were seen in the distance, Matilda Carter behind the rest. The child ran along the road, passing the others, and not stopping till she had reached Mattie, to whom she had taken a great fancy.

The young women were affectionately welcomed by Elsie Dale. Entering the comfortable little parlour, they saw that the table was spread for tea. Elsie had done her best to make it a good one. The kettle was boiling on the hob, and an old man and woman, Elsie's parents, sat one on each side of the fire-place, in their cushioned arm-chairs. These worthy people might well be considered chimney ornaments, and very pretty ones too! The old lady was knitting socks with a peaceful look in her calm grey eyes, her silvery locks put neatly back under a white frilled cap, and a little shawl crossed over her chest. Elsie's father, too, was a picture of happy old age, as he leaned upon his stick and listened with interest to what the young people had to say, occasionally putting in a cheery word. He had sparkling black eyes, and his hair was as white as time could make it.

The old people were always pleased to see Elsie's friends, most of whom, like herself, belonged to Mrs. Lester's Bible-class.

Elsie was very good to her parents. She watched over them tenderly and carefully, and saw that they wanted for nothing, being only too glad it was in her power to supply any *extra* need, for they were not dependent upon her.

William Dale, for many years, had been head gardener to some gentleman of property, and had laid by money, with part of which he bought the cottage where the Dales lived at the time of which I write, thinking that thus Elsie would have a home, and be so far provided for when he and her mother would be removed by death. They came to live at Wilminster to be near their married daughter. The old man was seldom able to go out to work now, but he enjoyed attending to his own little garden, and to the potatoes and vegetables in the plot of ground at the back of the house.

He and his wife seemed to be stepping down towards the river of death, hand-in-hand, but they went on calmly and fearlessly, for they trusted the promise, "When thou passest through the waters, I will be with thee;" and though the dear old people knew not what to expect when they thought of the "many mansions" of the Heavenly Father's House, yet they felt sure a glad surprise awaited them, and that everything in that peaceful home would be more grand and beautiful than they could think; and the best of all was the sweet thought that their Lord and Saviour would be with them. So the brightness which shone upon them from beyond the river cheered on the aged pilgrims, and made them think little of the cold waters which flowed between them and the "land of pure delight" to which they were hastening.

Although Elsie never neglected her parents nor her niece, and had sometimes to work rather hard at her dressmaking, yet she contrived now and then to make an opportunity for paying Helen Stacey a visit, or for reading to "blind Thomas" or "Widow Allen," and these visits were dearly prized.

When tea was over, old William Dale strolled out of doors and Mrs. Dale busied herself in the kitchen. Minnie took away the tea things, Mattie helping her; then print and other materials were placed on the table, and Elsie began to show the girls how to cut out and make children's frocks, pinafores, and other garments.

The secret of it all was that those who belonged to Mrs. Lester's Bible-class, and had some leisure time during the week, made little articles of clothing to sell in a missionary basket. Elsie Dale, being a dressmaker, was well able to help those less practised in needlework than herself.

It took some time to put them in the way of their work, and then all were eager to tell what had interested them of late, to speak of their troubles and difficulties, and of their friends at home. This varied information was poured into Elsie's sympathising ears.

She would never encourage them to mention the private concerns of their masters and mistresses, as that would have been a breach of confidence, and therefore dishonourable. Her advice was always wise and practical, and invariably given in a loving way, however hard to follow it might seem at the time. Occasionally she would contribute a little help in the shape of money to those who might be in need.

"I have not seen you at the class lately, Hattie," said Elsie. "Have you not been able to come, dear?"

"Well, Auntie, a friend of mine asked me to walk

with her, and I did not like to refuse last Sunday, as it was so fine."

"Oh, that was rather a pity! Could you not have walked with her another time?"

"Now, Hattie, what have you to say for yourself? You know you've been a regular truant for several Sundays," said Mary Smith with a mischievous smile.

Poor Harriet's lame excuses went for nothing with her companions, but she promised "Auntie," as the younger girls were in the habit of calling Elsie, that she would go to Mrs. Lester's the next Sunday.

"That's right, dear," said Elsie; "I like to see your face amongst the rest. You may not always have the opportunity of attending the class, you know," she added.

"No, to be sure not, Auntie, and I like going to it very well."

"So do I," exclaimed Elsie. "It's a privilege I wouldn't miss if I could help. I've been trying to get some more girls to join," she continued, "but it's not that easy to persuade people to do what is best for themselves; perhaps in time they may come round to being willing to go. I don't mean to give them up at present, for I'm a pertinacious creature."

"Auntie, have you heard that Annie Bennett is ill?" asked Harriet Westbrook.

"Yes; Mrs. Lester told me last Sunday. She's

had that cough so long, poor girl! I'm not surprised, but I'm very sorry. If I can possibly find leisure, I shall go over and see her soon. She's such a bashful little thing! I hope I may be able to make friends with her."

"Do you think there'll be much for the basket this year?" asked Fanny Lawrence.

"I really cannot say," said Elsie. "There are so few now in the class who have opportunity for working at missionary things. Lady Dalby's maid told me that when the company was gone she would be more at liberty for it."

"How grand and stiff she is!" said Fanny. "I feel as if I must make myself scarce when I see her come into the room. She seems to look down upon us all. Why can't she be one of us?"

"She does give herself airs!" said Harriet.

"I know her manner is trying," observed Elsie, "but we won't talk against her; she's had a great deal of trouble. I think we ought rather to pity than blame her."

"Auntie's a rare one for making the best of people," exclaimed Hattie Westbrook.

"Emma is saving money to buy materials to be made up for the basket," said Elsie.

"Doesn't Mrs. Lester find the materials, Auntie?" asked Fanny.

"Yes, she does; but then it is nice to help a wee

bit in the way of money as well as work, if one can manage it. Julia saves up odds and ends of silk and ribbon to make needle-cases and pin-cushions. She is a clever little body."

"I should like to be one to take the basket round," said Mary Smith. "I wonder whether my mistress could spare me. I'll ask her, that I will."

"It's pleasant to do anything to help forward a good work, isn't it?" said Elsie.

"Yes, it's sweet to do it for *Him*," remarked Mary with reverence, and half aloud.

"That's it, dear; and He doesn't mind its being a small thing, if it's all we can do."

"Mrs. Lester talked of having a working party once a quarter," put in Matilda. "She said she wanted us to come to tea, and she would read to us some interesting stories of the missionaries and the people they go amongst."

"That would be nice!" the girls exclaimed.

"Yes, I heard her say so too," said Fanny; "but she told us she wouldn't have any one to make even a trifle for the missionary basket instead of doing that which her mistress expected her to do."

"Neither would she have any one take home work to finish who had only time enough to keep her own clothes tidy," said Matilda.

"Oh no!" remarked Elsie. "I am quite sure Mrs. Lester would not wish any girl to encroach

on her mistress's time, however good the cause
might be for which she used her needle, nor to
neglect her own work; still sometimes, with a
little effort, girls can do more than they would
think, for 'where there's a will there's a way.'"

Much cheerful chat followed this conversation,
and all were very merry. Then Elsie said—

"I know you will be wanting to go soon, don't
you think it would be nice to read a few verses of
Scripture, and have a prayer together before we
part ?"

"Yes, *I* do," Mary Smith replied with earnestness.

"Should we sing that hymn first, Auntie, 'Work,
for the night is coming?'" suggested Fanny.

To this Elsie willingly agreed; and then, when the
singing was ended, she read 2 Corinthians viii., and
Mary, at her request, led the rest in a few simple words
of prayer. After this Minnie put some cakes on the
table with great pride and pleasure, as they were
her own making, and she brought in some mead
made by her aunt.

"I am always glad," said Mary, "that those people
you read about who were very poor and afflicted, and
yet gave so liberally to help others,—I do like to
think *they first gave themselves to the Lord !*"

"Yes; and therefore the love they showed was
Christian love. That was how they came to give so
liberally. The Lord Himself has set us the great

example of giving, as I read in the ninth verse. He gave Himself for us, and how much it cost Him to do so! Surely we ought to give ourselves to Him, and to His work as well, so far as He points out the way!"

"Mother used always to take us to missionary meetings when she could," Matilda said. "She often told us how hard it was that there should be so many poor heathen people in the world, and yet that Christians shouldn't do as much as they could to teach them what's good."

"Your mother was quite right, Mattie. If we've been so much better off, and have heard of the Saviour all our lives, it does seem cruel if we don't do what we can to let the poor idolaters know about Him!" observed Mary.

"Yes, indeed!" said Elsie; "and we have the Bible, which they have not. Each of us remembers our Saviour's command, 'Go ye into all the world, and preach the gospel to every creature.'"

"But," said Fanny Lawrence, "*we* cannot go out to preach the gospel."

"No, dear; but we can all do something, or give something, to help to send out the missionaries. Those of us who love the Lord Jesus must wish to obey Him and make Him known to those who have never heard about Him."

"Yes; and we can pray for them and the missionaries too," added Mary.

The girls then put on their hats, and wished good-bye to the old people, who had come back into the parlour. After affectionate farewells to Elsie and Minnie, the young women set out in the direction of their various places, as it was growing dusk, and the dew was falling; bats had begun to describe circles in the air, and cockchafers to wheel their "droning flight."

We too must say Good-night to Elsie Dale till the following chapter, in which some account will be given of her.

CHAPTER III.

"The Shepherd sought his sheep,
The Father sought His child;
They followed me o'er vale and hill,
O'er deserts waste and wild.
They found me nigh to death,
Famished, and faint, and lone;
They bound me with the bands of love,
They saved the wandering one.
They spoke in tender love,
They raised my drooping head,
They gently closed my bleeding wounds,
My fainting soul they fed."—BONAR.

ELSIE DALE was the youngest of the family, and a great pet with her parents, long before the time that she could first run to their knees and nestle in their arms. She was several years younger than her only remaining brother, who came between her and her sister. As the little girl grew older she became the sunbeam of the house, and often by her winning ways beguiled her parents of their cares. When Elsie was about fifteen years of age it was thought well that she should go into service and learn housework. A place was found for her with a lady who knew her mother, and where Elsie had every prospect of being comfortable and cared for. The upper housemaid was to teach her her work.

Elsie was as blithe as a bee and as playful as a kitten, and soon made friends. Though the first few nights after leaving home she cried herself to sleep thinking of her father and mother, and the separation of six miles between her and them, and although she awoke in the morning with a load at her heart, still the girl's cheerful nature soon overcame the homesick feelings, and she worked with a will, resolving to learn what was expected of her as quickly as possible, in the hope of returning the sooner to her parents' roof.

Elsie was small for her age, and looked but a child, although she now wore longer dresses and a little cap. Having always been much petted, her innocent light-hearted manner caused her to be regarded as much younger than she was.

Elsie had, however, a failing which is by no means uncommon among young girls. Good-tempered, kind, and affectionate as she was, "sweet as spring flowers," her fond father would say, yet was she heedless, thoughtless, and forgetful.

Without the slightest intention of disobeying her mistress or any one else placed above her, Elsie yet did not take sufficient pains to remember her duties, did not *think over* what she had been told to do, or to avoid doing, did not *connect it in her mind with something else*, in order that she could not possibly forget it; therefore she was often found fault with for neglecting things, or for not doing them in the way, or at the time she had been told.

Elsie had always the good grace to express her sorrow for having forgotten to do what was right, and many might copy her example in this respect with great advantage! but though this was well, and only proper, and perhaps all that could be done under the circumstances, yet it did not make up for her not having taken the trouble to remember.

Dear young servants, you wish to do your duty, but you may perhaps have bad memories, or you may never have learnt how to use these faculties, then take a hint:—"*Arrange in your minds what you have to remember*," making one thing follow upon another in order of time, and "*learn it all off by heart*." Write it down on slips of paper to keep in your pockets, if you will, and do not forget to look at them occasionally; but it will be better for you to try to *remember* your duties. Look forward and ask yourselves what you have to recollect. Do not allow yourselves to go off into dreams, but get up and do something when you feel that you are beginning to give way to this idleness of mind, which will almost certainly lead to forgetfulness of duty.

To return to Elsie. One day some furniture had to be moved out of a bedroom, and her help was required. She was, though small, a strong, healthy girl, and proud of her strength. Having forgotten that her mistress had been particular in telling her not to carry anything very heavy downstairs by herself, she caught up a rather small, but heavily-laden box. The servant she was helping called out, "Put that down, Elsie; it's too much for you alone."

Elsie, however, exclaiming, "It's nothing! I can lift heavier weights than this," went briskly to the stairs with her burden, holding it by the strap which fastened it. On descending she felt it was beyond her strength, and in trying to turn and rest it on a step it hit against the wall, her foot slipped, the box pushing her down, and falling with her.

A cry between a shriek and a moan, and poor Elsie lay senseless at the bottom of the staircase. The terrified servant, trembling with fright, hastened down, and there was a rush from several quarters to see what was the matter.

"Stop, Hannah," said her mistress, with a face white with apprehension. "We will not raise her till we know what mischief is done, for fear of increasing it."

With as gentle a touch as could be, Mrs. Masters discovered that the poor girl's leg was broken. The cook had come forward, and she offered her help in carrying Elsie to the sofa in the breakfast-room, which was near.

"I think it would be better to place her on a mattress, and take her to the blue-room at once," said Mrs. Masters.

This was a bedroom half-way up the stairs. Hannah and Wilson, Mrs. Masters' maid, ran to fetch a small mattress, on which Elsie was carefully placed and carried up, but the movement recalled sufficient consciousness to make her groan with pain. The bed was soon made ready, whilst Mrs. Masters, with Hannah's help, undressed the unconscious girl, so as to move her as little as possible. Then, with the cook's assistance, she was skilfully lifted into bed. This was scarcely accomplished when the doctor, who had been sent for, arrived. He found that Elsie's right leg was badly broken. After he had made various inquiries about the fall, Hannah told him that the box had struck Elsie's back, but not her head, which was true; there was no injury of consequence there, but harm had been done to the spine. When the fractured bone was set, Dr. Eden told Mrs. Masters he feared it would be a tedious business. His patient could not be moved for a length of time.

Mrs. Masters wrote to Elsie's mother, telling her of the accident as gently as might be, and requesting her to come at once to nurse her daughter. The

note was entrusted to the driver of the fly sent to
fetch Mrs. Dale. The parents were greatly shocked
and distressed. Dale came with his wife to learn
particulars and see his child, and then walk home.

It was a long, sad nursing. Elsie for a while
after the accident was insensible. As consciousness
gradually returned she wondered what had happened, how it was that she was in the blue-room,
and why her mother was there. On being reminded,
a dim recollection came to her of falling downstairs,
but of nothing more. It was, of course, very pleasant to have her mother with her, but Elsie found
the pain she suffered hard to bear. The doctor
had said he feared it would be a considerable time
before the poor girl would be well, but she was to be
taken home as soon as her leg would permit.

Mrs. Masters and her family were very kind to
Elsie, and all that could be thought of to add to
her comfort was cheerfully done. Mrs. Dale was
truly sorry that her dear child should be such a
tax upon their kindness. Elsie often said that she
would serve Mrs. Masters for nothing when she
should be well again.

As the injured leg recovered, Elsie began to sit
up, but the pain in her back soon put a stop to
this; so she was partially dressed and laid on her
bed during the day. How stiff her leg was when
she tried to use it! and how it hurt her back to

move about! Elsie was to have crutches, but she hoped soon to be able to do without them, and to skip along as before. She was counting much on seeing her father and brother again. Her sister, ten years older than herself, had been married for the last two years and was living at a distance.

At length the day arrived for Elsie to go home. She was dressed ready for the journey and laid down, when the various members of the household came to say good-bye.

Little Elsie was sadly altered. The roses had faded from her cheeks, her eyes looked large and told of suffering, and she was much wasted.

Mrs. Masters sat some time with her that morning whilst all was being packed up. She lent the invalid some interesting books, and promised to drive over and see her; which pleased her not a little. Mrs. Dale tried to speak her thanks for all the kindness shown to her and Elsie, but she felt what she could not express.

The poor child seemed more composed than any one else, and, in return for the kind words and kisses of the servants, as they took a sympathising farewell, she fondly held their hands and faintly smiled. As she was lifted into the carriage, across which a board had been placed with cushions, there were tears in other eyes than her mother's. A large bouquet of flowers was brought by one of the young ladies, and many things which might prove comforts to Elsie were placed in the carriage ere it drove off.

As may be supposed, the six-mile drive was very trying to her, but how delightful it was, notwithstanding the pain she was enduring, to see her father and Jack again,—especially the former.

He had counted the days till his young daughter should come home, but he had not expected to find such an alteration in her. He could scarcely restrain his feelings till he had helped her out of the carriage, and laid her on the sofa in the sitting-room. Then she clasped his neck, and kissed him many times.

" Oh dear ! " she exclaimed; " what shall I do ? my back is bad ! never mind. It's sure to be better soon."

" My poor child ! " was all the father could say at first, and the hot tears fell on Elsie's little white face.

" Oh, dad, dear, don't cry," she said, looking frightened and distressed. " I've come here to get well. My leg is all right now, only it's rather stiff, and it hurts me to use it as I ought, because of the pain in my back."

Then followed more kisses.

" Let me go now, my darling; I won't be out long. You haven't seen Jack yet."

" Well, wife, how are you ? I'm glad enough to have you home again," he said, kissing her; " but I didn't expect to see the child look like that."

"No; I dare say not, William; but I hope she's getting on, and the doctor who's attended her all along is coming here to see her. How are you, father? You don't look quite the thing!"

"Oh, I'm all right, thank you!" saying which, he hastily walked out of the house, and gave way to a fit of tears. "We've made an idol of our child," he said to himself; "she's going to be taken from us; she won't be here long, I can see."

However, the poor man soon roused himself, and after bathing his eyes at the pump, and pacing backwards and forwards two or three times, he came in again. Meanwhile the good mother found plenty to do in unpacking her own and Elsie's boxes, and putting things straight, whilst Jack addressed himself to his sister, of whom he was very fond. He was kind-hearted and amusing, and did what he could to brighten Elsie's return home. In spite of the pain in her back, she could not help a little laugh now and then at some of his odd speeches.

Their father soon returned, and then all had dinner; after which arrangements were made for Elsie to rest on the sofa in the kitchen during the day, and to be carried up to bed at night.

Poor girl! it was necessary for her to be laid on her back for a year or two, during which time she grew very fast, except, alas! the injured leg. When at last she was able to go about again, it was evident

that she would always require the help of crutches.
That interval of trial and suffering was not lost upon
her.

Elsie had been blessed with Christian parents, who
had earnestly sought to lead her to the Saviour. She
had been well taught from her earliest years, and had
always liked to hear of Jesus and His love, of heaven
and its blessedness, and of good things generally; but
notwithstanding, she was only what is called *well-
disposed*. The great change had not taken place.
Elsie had never trusted in Christ for salvation, and
had no real love for holiness: in fact a feeling of
dread and shrinking would come over her when
pressed to give herself to the Lord, and to take Him
for her Saviour. Amiable as she was, Elsie nevertheless shrank from self-denial, and looked upon true
religion as constant and painful cross-bearing; and
yet her parents by their lives had shown her how
much there was to admire in it, and that it rendered
them happy; but then, she thought, age made all
the difference. She hoped to be good some day,
and confessed to herself that she was not inclined
that way just then.

When Dale went off to his work, before leaving
the house he would stoop down and silently kiss his
young daughter. Rubbing his eyes with the back
of his hand, he would breathe an oft-repeated prayer
that her affliction might be blessed to her soul.

Elsie's mother was accustomed to read a portion of Scripture to her invalid child, night and morning, beside what was read at family prayers. Sometimes Mrs. Dale would make a remark, or press home some important truth, and, though Elsie would make no reply, she would think it over, having much opportunity for this. The hours often passed very slowly, and she was liable to become depressed.

Elsie had been feeling very low one evening when alone for a little while in the twilight. She had wondered whether she should ever be well and able to walk again, and had indulged in a quiet cry. The merry shouts of the village children outside the garden gate, and the fragrance of early summer flowers and new-mown hay came in from the open door and casement-window, for the front of the cottage was covered with roses and honeysuckle, and pretty meadows joined the well-kept garden. Oh! if she had but the use of her legs like those happy children. How the sweet-smelling flowers, which peeped at her round the lattice of the porch, seemed to tempt her to bound out of doors! The cool of the day was always such a pleasant time in summers gone by. The scent of the hay recalled childish pleasures.

Many times had Elsie reproached herself for her heedlessness, knowing she had no one else to blame for her crippled state. " But," she thought, " could

not God have prevented it? and, if so, why didn't
He?"

Her fond father had often called Elsie his "pet
lamb," and once "his wounded lamb," which words
remained in her memory, and had that day been
brought to mind over and over again with a feeling
of bitterness and rebellion against God.

Much kindness was shown to Elsie during her
season of trial. The clergyman, his wife, the ladies
from the hall, and others were accustomed to visit
and read to her, besides her own friends and young
companions. There seemed no want unsupplied by
those who loved and pitied her, except indeed the
want of all wants, that of the "one thing needful."

Mrs. Meredith, the lady from the Rectory, appeared at the open door that evening of which
I was speaking, when Elsie was alone in the
kitchen.

"Well, Elsie, may I come in?"

"Come in, ma'am, please. Can you find a seat?"

"Oh yes," was the reply, as Mrs. Meredith seated
herself by Elsie's couch, took her hand, and inquired,
"How are you to-day, my child?"

"Much the same as usual, ma'am, thank you. My
back gets painful if I move about. I don't attempt
to walk yet."

"Still I hope you suffer less than you did when
first you came home?"

"Yes, ma'am; maybe I do; but it's slow work, and time seems to hang heavy."

After talking kindly and pleasantly for a few minutes, Mrs. Meredith offered to read to Elsie. Opening the little Bible she had brought with her, the lady read from the 11th to the end of the 16th verses of the xxxiv. chapter of Ezekiel. "Elsie," she said, "the Good Shepherd has been seeking you. Has He found the lost sheep?"

Elsie did not reply, but turned her face away and looked uncomfortable.

"We are all naturally very far from Christ," Mrs. Meredith went on to say. "We do not love Him, nor care to please Him, nor wish to be holy. The longer we live the greater the distance becomes between us and Him, for our sins, like dark mountains, separate us farther and farther from God. We are by nature 'lost,' but the Lord Jesus came 'to seek and to save' the lost, or you and I would perish in hell without the slightest hope of escape being held out to us. What cause for thankfulness that He comes to us as we are, in our sins, to raise us by His almighty power! He will rejoice to carry us safely home if we will only let Him. Elsie, He has lifted me up, will you not let Him take you and make you His,—His happy child,—His folded sheep?" Mrs. Meredith paused, but as the sick girl made no attempt to speak, continued, reminding her how "King David was once a shepherd, and therefore knew well what sheep wanted, and how to take care of them. He felt that he too needed a shepherd, not only to supply his bodily wants, but those also of his soul, and David was so happy as to be able to say, 'The LORD is my Shepherd,' and he could therefore add, 'I shall not want,' or according to the prayer-book, 'therefore can I lack nothing.' I fancy, dear, you do not always feel quite satisfied to lie here, whilst others are actively employed, and you, perhaps, in pain. It must be very trying!"

The colour rushed to Elsie's cheeks, and her eyes filled with tears. "Indeed, ma'am," she said, "I have been wishing, as I often do, that I could get about like other people."

"Well, my child, I hope you will be able to do so some day; that is, with the help of crutches. Still, even now, if the LORD were your Shepherd, you might, by His grace, be content and happy that His will should be done, and able to say, 'I shall not want,' 'I can lack nothing.'"

Mrs. Meredith then spoke of the *rest of heart* which the "Good Shepherd" gave David, "He maketh me to lie down,"—of the *food for his thoughts* in the "green pastures," the sweet promises of God in Christ, which are always satisfying to those who take them for their own. She dwelt upon the *refreshment* of the water of life, the Holy Spirit revealing the Saviour just according to the need felt, and in all His love, and power, and grace, and entreated Elsie to pray for the Holy Spirit's teaching, asking her to repeat the promise in St. Luke xi. 13. Then Mrs. Meredith touched upon the further blessings which David recounted as the happy consequences of having the LORD for his shepherd, especially that of *deliverance from the fear of evil*, because the Almighty Friend, in whose presence He rejoiced, would remain with him, cheering him with the assurance of His protecting care, warding off evil as a shepherd's crook would serve to drive away wolves and savage beasts, and comforting him by the sweet support the Word of God holds out, like a staff to bear up the soul under trial, or Elsie's crutches, when she would be able to walk by leaning upon them. "David," Mrs. Meredith remarked, "*risked his life* in defending his father's sheep from the lion and the bear, but the great Shepherd of His people *laid down His life* for the sheep. Must it not be a good thing to have the Lord Jesus Christ for our shepherd, Elsie?"

"Yes, ma'am, it must," was the whispered reply.

"I think He has allowed all this pain and trouble to come, in order that you may be willing to let Him take you up in the arms of His love, and so save the wounded lamb; but listen to what I read in Ezekiel, 'I will bind up that which is broken, and will strengthen that which is sick.'"

D

Mrs. Meredith then spoke of the Lamb of God
who was "wounded for our transgressions," dying
on the cross that we might be healed of sin and have
everlasting life, and that this great cure is effected
by the look of simple, earnest faith raised to the
Lord Jesus; just as the Israelites in the wilderness,
bitten by serpents, had but to look up to the brazen
serpent to be healed. Mrs. Meredith then wished
Elsie "good evening."

Many times did the young girl think over all that
had been said, and after her father had carried her
up to bed, and her parents had wished her "good
night," she still lay pondering and reflecting about
it, and how it was so strange that Mrs. Meredith
should call her a "wounded lamb," the very words
which had haunted her all day; Elsie had almost
started when she heard them. She had felt much
happier since the lady had called. The bitter feeling
was gone.

Elsie knew she had "erred and strayed from God's
ways" like a lost sheep, and felt the need of what
the Good Shepherd, the Lamb of God, could do for
her; tears of penitence filled her eyes when she
called to mind how hardly she had thought of Him;
but it did seem so great a thing to put herself into
His hands; she shrank from it, scarcely knowing
why, yet having a secret hope that He was seeking
her, a wounded lamb! Elsie asked for the Holy

Spirit, and day by day became increasingly conscious how greatly she needed the Saviour.

At last a time came when she was overcome by a sight of the love of Christ, whilst studying "the words of eternal life." That love suited her need as exactly as a key fits into its lock. She was encouraged by a sweet hope, and felt she could no longer live without Him. A grateful adoration, quite new to her, filled her heart, and the words of the hymn expressed her state:

> " I could not do without Thee,
>   O Saviour of the lost,
>   Whose precious blood redeem'd me
>   At such tremendous cost;
>   Thy righteousness, thy pardon,
>   Thy precious blood must be
>   My only hope and comfort,
>   My glory and my plea.
>
>   I could not do without Thee;
>   No other friend can read
>   The spirit's strange deep longings,
>   Interpreting its need;
>   No human heart could enter
>   Each dim recess of mine,
>   And soothe, and hush, and calm it,
>   O blessèd Lord, but Thine."

Elsie took Him as her Saviour, and the Good Shepherd raised the wounded lamb and carried her in His bosom.

Shortly afterwards she spoke of what had taken

place in this way, " Mother, dear, I've something to say to you. I am so happy now."

" Are you, my darling? What makes you happy?" said Mrs. Dale, hoping, with trembling anxiety, that the answer to her many prayers had come.

" I've seen the love of the Lord Jesus in dying for me as I've never seen it before, and I can trust Him. He's *my* Saviour now, mother."

" My precious child! How can I be thankful enough!" and her mother kissed Elsie with tears of grateful joy.

Then Elsie related all about Mrs. Meredith's visit, and what had passed in her own mind since, adding that she hoped the lady would soon come again to see her.

" How rejoiced father will be to hear it!" the mother said.

His thankfulness was expressed in leading his wife and daughter in simple but hearty words of praise and prayer.

Now Elsie could bear her trial patiently, and even cheerfully, for she cast her burden upon the LORD, and He sustained her.

After a while, Elsie's spine began to recover, and at the end of two years from the time of the accident, with the help of crutches, she was able to move about pretty comfortably. Well was it for her that, amongst other necessary things, she had learnt to sew neatly when a little girl at school! She was clever with her needle, and began to take in work, with which many kind friends were glad to supply her.

Presently it occurred to her to learn what she could of dressmaking, so, for a year or more, Elsie went daily to assist the village dressmaker.

Her niece, Minnie, had not long gone to live with her grandparents and aunt when they moved to Wilminster. She was a nice, bright girl, and her grandfather soon felt he could not do without her. He dearly loved to have some one to pet, and would say, "She's a child to be proud of, I'm very partial to her; but no one can come up to what her Aunt Elsie was, at her age."

This same Elsie has been the comfort of her parents in their declining years. Her own life has not been unhappy, notwithstanding her lameness and consequent privations. How could it be so, when she, by faith, could realise that around her were the "everlasting arms" of the Good Shepherd?

Happiness has been said to consist in the constant pursuit of some worthy object. Elsie set before her the highest possible object, the noblest aim, either for human beings on earth or for angels in heaven,— the honour of her Saviour and her God, the seeking to do or bear His will in all things. This she felt was worth living for. It was Christ-like, for had

not the Lord Jesus said, " I came down from heaven,
not to do mine own will, but the will of Him that
sent me "? (S. John vi. 38). In humble dependence
upon Him who alone could work in her " both to
will and to do of His good pleasure," Elsie did not
fail in her object in life, and she shared the Saviour's
own joy. There was also a secondary purpose for
which she lived; it grew naturally out of her desire
for God's glory, and that was the good of others.
She, perhaps, little guessed the success granted her
in this matter, but the very pursuit of such an object
is happiness; and a day is coming when all these
treasured secrets will be revealed.

Elsie had her trials, but she could adopt the
words—

> " We expect a bright to-morrow;
>   All will be well;
> Faith can sing through days of sorrow,
>   All, all is well.
> On our Father's love relying,
> Jesus every need supplying,
> Or in living or in dying,
>   All must be well."

CHAPTER IV.

"Vain as the leaf upon the stream,
And fickle as a changeful dream."—SCOTT.

"How long halt ye between two opinions?"
—I KINGS xviii. 21.

"Choose you this day whom ye will serve."
—JOSHUA xxiv. 15.

HARRIET WESTBROOK was one of the girls who met to work for the missionary basket, at Elsie Dale's. She was amiable, but of a weak disposition; very easily led either for good or for evil. She seemed to have no backbone of determination in her character, but was like a plant which bows before every wind that blows, being changeable, undecided, and indolent in mind. She lived at home with her grandmother, a good old woman, who was very fond of Hattie, and possessed much influence over her.

There were times when the girl would allow herself to be drawn away by one or more worldly companions, and, to the grief of her grandmother, she would go to scenes of folly and recklessness, where

God's Holy Name was taken in vain; or she would
join in very doubtful pleasures, where she could not
but witness much that her conscience told her was
wrong.   Then, on the other hand, Harriet has several
times been under strong religious impressions, when
she has shown a decision and purpose in the right
direction quite unusual to her, but, after a time, her
nature, " unstable as water," has given way again.
What an awfully dangerous thing it is to let religious impressions pass away disregarded! each
succeeding one will probably be more feeble than
the last, and, if resisted, will leave the heart harder
than before.

Some characters are weaker than others, and like
the ivy, they want supporting.   Christ alone can be
to them an unfailing support; and who does not
need that Tower of Strength?   Harriet sought not
His help; she did not lean upon Him.

A young man, whom she had known all her life,
had several times paid her attention, contrary to the
wishes of her grandmother, who would never hear of
a friendship between them, but had always given
him the " cold shoulder," knowing that he was
addicted to drink.   The worthless young man then
sought Harriet's company on the sly.   For a while
she avoided him, for she was fond of her grandmother, and did not wish to displease her.   Richard,
however, contrived one day to meet Hattie in a lane,

and asked her to marry him. She declined in a hesitating kind of manner, which made him press his suit the more earnestly. Harriet mentioned his drinking habits, when Richard said that she would be the saving of him, if she would consent to become his wife. He would promise to give up drink, and they would be so happy together.

The foolish girl yielded, as the young man offered to speak to her grandmother on the subject, and engaged to bring her round; but she would not hear a word about it, nevertheless Harriet and Richard met and walked together. The end of it was that they were married, and a wretched marriage it proved.

Just at first it was all very well, but before long, Richard again gave way to drink, and he was soon as bad as ever. Harriet tried to make a little money by taking in washing, for her husband's wages were chiefly spent at the public-house. In a short time she looked very different to the Hattie Westbrook of former days. All the brightness seemed gone from her young life. Her faded cheeks and hollow eyes made Harriet look years older. She appeared to lose hope and self-respect. The many efforts of kind friends to bring about a better state of affairs were apparently in vain. The poor old grandmother became almost broken-hearted.

What a comfort it is to know, even when things are at the very worst, either with ourselves or with those in whom we are interested, that we may still place them in the hand of God! and what cannot He accomplish?

This little story has its warning. How often a young woman's happiness for life, and perhaps also for eternity, has been wrecked by a want of decision and courage to do the right; by weakly yielding to entreaties, instead of turning a deaf ear to them from the first; by allowing herself to be talked over, against her convictions of duty, and contrary, it may be, to the expressed wishes of some parent or relative older and wiser than herself! She has not sought Heavenly guidance, or has not been willing to be guided by it, or has failed to seek the needed strength which would have enabled her to follow the gracious Guide, who would never have misled her. "Trust in the LORD with all thine heart; and lean not unto thine own understanding. In all thy ways acknowledge Him, and He shall direct thy paths" (Prov. iii. 5, 6).

CHAPTER V.

"Oh, what a tangled web we weave
When first we practise to deceive!"
—Scott.

ONE day Matilda Carter was walking with the children on the Hilton Road, when a young woman hurried past them without looking up.

"Why, that's Caroline!" exclaimed one. "How ill she looks!"

"I shouldn't have known her," said another.

Miss Lillie was half inclined to run on and speak to her, but Matilda thought their Mama would rather she did not follow her former nursemaid, considering the reason for which she had left them. They turned to watch in what direction she went; she was, however, soon out of sight.

"Poor Caroline! I wonder where she lives now," said Miss Lillie. "She did look ill and miserable, and no mistake!"

"Next time we come this way we'll keep a lookout after her," said Matilda, who longed to do something to help the unhappy girl, but had no idea how to be useful to her. "Tell your Mama about her when you get home, Miss Lillie. I should like to see if I can do anything for Caroline. It was so sad to catch sight of her looking like that!"

"Yes, I mean to tell Mama."

Mrs. Turner was sorry to hear the poor account of Caroline which her little girls gave her, and wrote at once to the stepmother hoping to learn where the young servant was living; but no answer came. The letter had been misdirected, and was returned. For some time to come the children went almost every day, with one or both of their nurses, on the Hilton Road, in hope of seeing Caroline again.

At last, one morning, they thought they caught a glimpse of her at a bedroom window, but the face was withdrawn immediately. Should they ask if she was there? Esther rang the bell. The landlady appeared, looking most forbidding.

"If you please, ma'am, will you tell me whether Caroline Hall lives here?" Esther asked.

"She does."

"Can I speak to her for a minute?"

"She's particularly engaged. I can give a message for you."

"Would you let her come to Mrs. Turner's as soon as you can spare her? She knows where."

"I'll see about it."

They withdrew as the woman closed the door against them. Day after day the children watched for Caroline, and wondered whether she would come. As she did not make her appearance, Mrs. Turner wrote to her, saying that she was sorry to hear from the young ladies and their nursemaid that Caroline was looking ill when they met her six or eight weeks past. Mrs. Turner would be glad to see her, and to hear how she liked her situation.

About a week after Caroline had received the letter, she went to her late mistress, who was shocked at the alteration in her. It was not only that she had become distressingly thin, white, and hollow-eyed, but it was the expression of helpless misery on her face which struck the lady most painfully. Caroline had endeavoured to make herself tidy, but even in that respect she was very different from what she had been. She curtsied and tried to smile. Mrs. Turner expressed her sorrow at seeing her look so far from well. The poor girl burst into tears. She had had little time or opportunity latterly for giving way to grief, neither had she dared to do so. Therefore a dull feeling of despair had taken possession of her; but a word and look of sympathy broke her down, and for some minutes she could not restrain her sobs.

Mrs. Turner spoke kindly and gently to Caroline, and found that she was very unhappy and over-

worked in her present place, but that she had given
her mistress a month's notice a few days before.
Her wages were small, but Mrs. Simpson's plan was,
to owe her servant some portion of them, in order to
prevent her leaving.

In the uncertainty of what was best to be done,
having had very little leisure to attend to herself,
and not wishing to go home, Caroline had remained
on where she was.

"Poor girl!" said Mrs. Turner, "it was indeed
a sad pity you were so untruthful, and had to leave
us!"

"Many's the time I've wished myself back again,
ma'am; but I dared not think too much about it."

"I suppose your father cannot have known that
you were not comfortable nor happy?"

"No, ma'am; I didn't wish to trouble him, so I
never told him when I wrote."

"But why did you not? He would have advised
and helped you."

"Well, ma'am, the fact was this: the last of my
being at my father's, my stepmother and I had some
words together, and though he knew nothing about
it, I resolved I would do anything rather than go
home again, for a long while to come."

"Oh, I am sorry there should be such a reason to
keep you away! I will do what I can to help you
to find a more comfortable place."

" Thank you kindly, ma'am."

" I hope, Caroline, you are really trying, with God's help, to be more truthful," and Mrs. Turner had some kind and faithful conversation with her former nursemaid, which was the means of calling forth in her heart more earnest desire after better things.

Though naturally timid, Caroline's spirit was sometimes roused, and then she could be very determined; this had been the case with regard to her stepmother, when, on being dismissed from Mrs. Turner's, she felt she could not and would not go home, much as she would have liked to have seen her father. Therefore after several efforts to obtain a better situation, the poor girl had accepted a most uncomfortable one in a lodging-house, where she was a complete drudge, toiling away from early morning till late at night without cessation. No wonder that she grew thin, and pale, and heavy-eyed! Her mistress was ill-tempered, exacting, and suspicious. Caroline met with little kindness and no sympathy. Fear drove her to her work, and kept her up to it. How deeply she regretted having brought upon herself so disgraceful a discharge from her former comfortable place of service. She often tried to ward off the angry words of her mistress at some accident or fault of hers, by saying what was untrue; but whenever she did so, her conscience pricked her sorely, for it had been awakened on different occasions by Mrs. Turner's faithful teaching respecting the sin and danger of deceit and falsehood.

Before returning, she was allowed to visit the nursery. The children and she were pleased to meet again, though appearing rather shy and constrained at first. Esther was kind and sympathising, Matilda very glad to see Caroline, and become in some measure acquainted with her.

A week after this Caroline caught a chill, and went to bed shivering, and feeling quite ill. Her sleep, which was only at intervals, was restless and feverish. She rose in the morning with an effort, felt wretched and depressed, but tried to do her work as usual, yet had neither energy nor strength. It was not long before she was found unconscious on the floor.

Her mistress was somewhat alarmed, and, by the advice of a lady lodging in the house, sent for a doctor. After a while Caroline was sufficiently recovered to be helped upstairs and laid down on her bed. As the doctor considered it a serious case, Mrs. Simpson decided to send her home at once, and despatched a note to Hall, asking him to fetch his daughter, as she had been taken very ill.

The village of Selbridge, where he lived, was only a mile and a half distant. The poor man was very troubled at receiving such news, and immediately

started to walk over, knowing that he should be able
to have a lift on his way. He was soon with Caroline, who was in a half-conscious state. Her mistress
promised that she should be wrapped up and prepared
to go, whilst he went for a fly. The lady lodger
kindly gave her assistance, put a warm shawl of her
own on Caroline, and persuaded her to swallow a
few spoonfuls of milk before leaving. Her father
carried her downstairs and placed her in the fly, and
they were soon at their journey's end, he supporting
her all the way.

Mrs. Hall came out to help when the carriage
stopped. She had been busy arranging all things in
readiness to receive her patient, evidently intending
to do her best and be kind. She was shocked to see
the alteration in Caroline, and softened in manner,
but the latter was too ill then to take much notice of
anything.

Meanwhile Mrs. Turner had been exerting herself
to do what she could for her. The lady sent a line
by post, asking Caroline to come and see her, thinking she had met with a situation to suit; but as the
poor girl neither came nor wrote, a servant was sent
to Mrs. Simpson's with a message, and was told that
Caroline had been taken home ill a week before.
Mrs. Turner was truly sorry, but not surprised, to
hear this. She determined to drive to Selbridge
and inquire after her, and found that Caroline was

E

extremely ill—too ill to see her, and would have to be kept perfectly quiet; and, in fact, that life seemed to hang in the balance.

Her stepmother was attentive to her wants, and felt more kindly to her than she had ever done before. During the weary hours of watching, conscience told Mrs. Hall that she had not been as considerate as she might have been to the motherless girl. What if she should die? The last interview between them before her illness had been so unpleasant, and would leave a most painful recollection behind. The anxious woman hoped indeed that Caroline might be spared, and that they might be more comfortable together in future.

At last the crisis came, as the doctor had foretold. Edmund Hall and his wife both watched the poor sufferer in painful suspense. Hour after hour went by, and neither had the heart to speak. At length the restless moanings, tossings, and delirium gave way, and Caroline sank into a long and peaceful sleep.

"Thank God!" sobbed out her father, "the worst is over, Missis. Poor little Carrie will do now."

"Oh! what a relief this is!" gasped out his wife.

After her quiet slumber, Caroline awoke conscious and refreshed.

"Oughtn't I to be getting up?" she asked.

"No, my dear," said her stepmother. "Lie still, you're very weak yet."

"I feel ever so much better. I must have been asleep an age. It seems like weeks and months," she said faintly.

"You've had a beautiful sleep, dear; and now you must take all the nourishment you can, the doctor says. Mrs. Turner has sent you some nice jelly. I should like you to try it; which Caroline did, and soon dozed off again, with a strange and happy feeling of how kind her stepmother was to her. The sick girl made progress slowly but surely.

One day Mrs. Hall said, "My dear, we've not been on the best of terms; but now, I hope things will mend. It's never too late for that, they say. You and I are such different folk, but we must strive to be comfortable together."

"Oh yes, mother! You've been so very good in nursing me! We'll 'let bygones be bygones.' I know I havn't been all I ought to you."

"Well, I've thought a deal about that split we had before you went to Mrs. Turner's, and often have I been vexed with myself for the part I took in it."

"Never mind, mother. Our tempers were both up then. I hope we shall get on all right in future. Thank you for the care you've taken of me since I've been laid up, and for all the nursing and watching."

"You'll want more attention yet, my dear; so keep your thanks a little longer."

Whilst recovering from her illness, Caroline pondered over Mrs. Turner's words during the last interview with her many times. Light dawning in the mind of the invalid, led her to see how wrong she had been in yielding to falsehood and deceit. She began to consider the sinfulness of such ways in the sight of God, and to desire earnestly that the life He was restoring to her might be a new and better one. She became very anxious to have her sins forgiven. They were a burden on her conscience which daily grew heavier.

Caroline was delighted when Mrs. Turner called, and drank in eagerly what she then heard of the Lord Jesus, and His love, and His great salvation, so freely offered to her. The lady told her that her nursemaid, Matilda, would be pleased to come and sit with her, should she feel disposed to see her. Caroline was gratified at the girl's kind thought, and asked whether she could be spared to take a cup of tea with her the next day. Mrs. Turner willingly acceded to this, and, about four o'clock the following afternoon, Mattie made her appearance.

" How good of you to come ! " exclaimed Caroline.

" No, indeed," replied Matilda.   " I've to thank you for asking me to tea."

" But it was kind of you to think of coming to sit with a sick girl like me !   Mother's going to bring your tea up here, so we can have a cup together."

" Oh, that will be cosy ! "

It is unnecessary to relate the conversation that passed between them; how Mattie drew forth Caroline's confidence by her sympathising words and manner; how Caroline found herself telling Matilda of her anxieties about her soul, and of her desire to lead a holier life; nor need the story be repeated of Mattie's sudden conversion, which she told in the hope that it might help the anxious one to find peace. Mattie had made this, as afterwards each succeeding visit, a subject of prayer.

God had been preparing Caroline's heart to receive the truth. Mrs. Turner's words, her prayers, and readings of Scripture, with the explanations she had given, had all been helpful. Some things she had said and read would long be remembered, and would be still more helpful and comforting; yet it was not good Mrs. Turner who was to be the honoured means in God's hand of guiding Caroline into the open arms of the Saviour who was seeking her; but it was Mattie, the simple, warm-hearted young girl, who had long waited, and prayed, and watched for an opportunity of being useful to some other girl, by leading her into the state of blessing into which she had found herself so quickly introduced some months before. It was Mattie's homely words, which, winged by the Spirit of God, drew Caroline to the Resting-Place of faith, the Lord Jesus Christ. One day when the friends were sitting together, Caroline said—

"You wouldn't think, Matilda, how hard I find it always to say what is exactly true; but I do wish to be truthful. It's easy for you to speak the truth, I daresay; but you cannot think how difficult it is to keep to what is quite true when one's never been in the habit of it."

"It must be hard, I'm sure," said Mattie, with her ready sympathy; "but you do try?"

"Yes, that I do; and I often pray about it."

"You're sure then to have the help you want, for we have so many promises that prayer shall be answered. You know Who only is able to keep you true in your words and ways. We all have our faults, and need to trust the Lord Jesus to save us from giving in to them."

"O Matilda! you've been such a help to me! I shall never forget your kindness."

"You don't know, dear, how much pleasure it gives me to come and see you. I am so thankful God has heard my prayer, and has let me be of some little use to you."

"It's not *a little* that you've helped me, Mattie. We shall always be friends, shall we not?"

"Yes, I hope so."

"When once you begin to be deceitful," remarked Caroline, reverting to what she had said before, "you never know where to stop. To make your tale good, you have to tell so many stories, for fear of being found out. Untruthfulness has given me a deal of trouble, I assure you."

"It must have been terrible the worry of it, and very confusing; but you've done with it now."

"'Easier said than done.' As I was saying, it's the *habit* which it is so difficult to get rid of."

After a pause, Caroline asked, "Will you tell me about your mother, Matilda, if you don't mind?"

"Oh yes; I love to think of her! she was always good and kind, and she's gone to glory; but then comes the thought of the sad loss it's been to me; still I want you to know about her. I often wish I was more like her."

"I should think you were very like her, if the truth was known."

"No, indeed, I am not! I can remember her prayers, and how she used to talk to me about trusting the Lord, for Him to save me and keep me," and Mattie told Caroline much more.

It had indeed been a great advantage to Matilda that she had had a Christian mother for the first twelve years of her life, also that she had been taught much of Scripture! Poor Caroline felt her ignorance in this respect, and began trying to supply the deficiency, as far as possible, by learning chapters and verses by heart, and by regular reading of both Old and New Testaments.

She became more and more watchful over her

words, and if she found she had gone beyond the truth, or had given a false impression, she would stop and correct it. Twice, under strong temptation, Caroline again gave way to her besetting sin, which sad slips afterwards cost her many bitter tears, and made her more assured than ever that she could not trust herself. She was thus driven to place more entire confidence in the Saviour, to be kept from falling. Desiring to please Him, she sincerely wished to be true in both words and actions. Well would it be if all the followers of Christ realised, as she did, the great importance of being truthful!— the grievous sin of untruthfulness!

When Caroline was growing stronger, she went to spend a day at Mrs. Turner's. Happening to be alone with the children for a few minutes, she said very earnestly, "Master Walter, dear, mind you never say what is not quite true, even if it doesn't seem to hurt anybody. I was wrong, indeed, when I lived with you, in teaching you to be untrue; but I've learnt better now, and I am so sorry I ever said what I did."

CHAPTER VI.

"Let knowledge grow from more to more,
But more of reverence in us dwell."—TENNYSON.

"Let us have grace, whereby we may serve God acceptably with reverence and godly fear."—HEB. xii. 28.

THE town of Wilminster was all astir. Against many houses ladders had been placed, and men on them were suspending festoons of evergreens. Skeletons of triumphal arches had been previously erected in light wood-work; and now carts filled with branches of laurel and boughs of fir, might be seen in the streets, whilst men were covering these gateways with evergreens, and adding bright flowers and gay devices. Flags and mottoes were beginning to make the place look festive, and high poles with turnips to surmount them were being painted red and blue, in preparation for the banners which would float from them. Beautiful plants in pots were being arranged on balconies and other available places, to do their part in the general rejoicing. Many of the dwellings and shops in the High Street had been lately painted, in readiness for the occasion.

Shopkeepers were standing outside their premises to watch their decoration, and there were admiring groups of idlers in all directions. Flags were for sale, windows for hire, medals were struck, and brooches made, to commemorate the coming event. In open spaces where the grand procession would pass, raised seats had been erected two or three days beforehand, for the new Town Hall was to be opened by a royal personage.

Down a narrow street, where the houses varied in size and style, an old lady was giving instructions about the putting up of some wreaths of ivy intermixed with paper flowers. She felt obliged to ornament her house, for decorations were expected all along the line of route. She had begun to make these pink and yellow roses a month before, but happily they were not of a kind to fade.

Mrs. Storey kept a small milliner's shop. Her niece, Jane Bowman, lived with her, and helped in the business.

"I wondered what on earth had become of you, Jennie," said Mrs. Storey, addressing the girl, who hastily came up to where the old lady was standing, and appeared to be about sixteen years of age. "You shouldn't have left me so long. Where have you been?"

"Well, Aunt Eliza, I had such a lot to see after. Do just take a peep in the High Street; it's getting

on splendidly! You wouldn't know the place. Mr.
Parson says they'll make a first-rate concern of it.
Do you know they're making Joe paint the poles;
and you never saw such a state as he's in! As for
me, I've been here, there, and everywhere; and
really I hardly know whether I'm on my head or my
heels."

"How you rattle away! You might be more
considerate at your age. There's no one in the shop
if anybody should call; you must go and attend
to it."

"Oh! very well," said Jennie, in a discontented
tone, adding, in a lower voice, "I hate the old shop;"
whilst her aunt remarked to herself, "This fuss is
enough to turn the heads of the giddy girls of the
present time. How different things were in my
young days!" and the old lady sighed at the con-
trast which had probably grown in her memory and
imagination. She was rather over strict and particular with her niece, who had lived with her for the
last two years. The lively Jennie was not a bad-
intentioned girl, but too much inclined to be
flighty.

"Auntie," she said, "you'll go to the sports to-
morrow night, won't you? It'll do you so much
good."

"I hardly know, child. I think at my age I'm
best indoors when there's a merrymaking."

"O Aunt Eliza! at your tender years!"

"Come, Jennie, no nonsense. I don't mean to let you laugh at me about my age," said Mrs. Storey, looking annoyed. "That's an experiment that won't pay you."

"Well, Auntie, I don't mind so very much if you don't go to the sports, because the Walkers have promised to take me with them."

"Oh, indeed! Then why did you ask me? I'm not at all sure I shall let you go."

However, when Mrs. Walker called and asked permission, Mrs. Storey did not like to refuse her, and therefore Jennie went and thoroughly enjoyed herself.

The day was fine for all the grand doings. As usual on such occasions, the bells rang merry peals, soldiers lined the streets, and the procession passed whilst military bands were playing. Everything went off to the satisfaction of the inhabitants.

Mrs. Storey had asked Mrs. Lester to allow Jennie to attend her Bible-class. The girl was generally there, for she knew her aunt would inquire if this was the case; and as Jennie was very dependent upon Mrs. Storey, it would be most uncomfortable to offend her seriously. Jane Bowman was rather a troublesome member of the class, having never been taught in her earlier years much reverence, or even respect, for religion. She would try to make her companions laugh whilst managing to keep grave herself. Occasionally a whisper might be heard from her to the girl next her while the Bible lesson was going on, and even during the prayer. Of course this had to be stopped at once, but it would not be many Sundays before something else occurred of a similar. kind. Now and then Jennie's spirits would quite carry her away, and then the most trifling thing would upset her gravity.

More than once Mrs. Lester talked seriously to her on the sin of trifling in the special presence of God, and at last felt compelled to request her to give up coming to the class unless she meant to behave better, for her influence on others was so bad. At the same time the lady spoke kindly, and made allowance for Jane's lively nature. Quick-tempered as the girl was, and. inclined to resent any reproof, she yet could not do otherwise than take Mrs. Lester's words in good part, and she promised to be more careful over her conduct in future.

The Bible-class, however, was not the only place where Jane Bowman's irreverent behaviour was seen. On a Sunday, in the House of God, she would join some giddy companion, with whom she would laugh and whisper during the service and sermon, to the great disturbance of her neighbours. Sitting down and leaning over the book-desk during prayer was a favourable opportunity for whispering and exchanging notes. It never occurred to these girls that God could hear and see it all.

Jane's aunt, not being able to walk far, attended another place of worship, but friends acquainted her with her niece's conduct. Mrs. Storey was extremely annoyed, and gave her such a lecture as she never forgot, and requested Mrs. Lester to speak to her. The lady's kind and earnest remonstrance made a great impression upon Jane, who promised, with tears, to behave differently for the time to come.

"There is one verse," said Mrs. Lester, "that I should like you to learn by heart. I have written it out for you—'God is greatly to be feared in the assembly of the saints, and to be had in reverence of all them that are about Him'" (Psalm lxxxix. 7).

Occasionally Mrs. Lester would give a word of warning about the hymns sung at the class, asking the girls not to sing some solemn verses unless they could do so from the heart. "God knows how much is sincere," she would say; "He is not mocked. Do not sing the words unless they are true of *you*."

Jennie certainly was more quiet in the House of God after the reproofs she had had, especially as her aunt threatened to have her niece sit with her in church. The girl also became more attentive at the class. She was naturally quick, and soon showed more interest in the Bible lessons, and felt somewhat impressed by what she there heard.

Mrs. Storey had not been well for several days, and complained of headache. One morning she said—

"Jennie, I must have you go for Dr. Waters. I have such an oppression in my head."

"Very well, auntie; but let me bathe it first;" which she did.

"Thank you, my dear, that will do."

Jennie set down the sponge and basin, and hastened upstairs to put on her outdoor things. She was always glad of a little walk in the town, and to leave the dull shop, but this time she felt frightened about her aunt, having noticed a peculiar look in her eyes. Jennie walked quickly and reached the doctor's in about a quarter of an hour. She waited some minutes, as he had not come home, but was shortly expected. After telling him the state of the case, she speedily returned to her aunt, but on entering the parlour at the back of the shop, what was the poor girl's dismay to find Mrs. Storey lying senseless on the floor! Jennie knew, from her aunt's appearance, that there was reason to fear something worse than a fainting fit. No one was in the house but themselves. What could be done? Terrified and bewildered, Jane ran to tell Mrs. Walker next door. The good woman sent her boy to hasten the doctor, and then immediately followed Jennie. They did all they could for Mrs. Storey.

Dr. Waters was not long in coming, but to Jane every minute seemed a length of time. When he saw his patient he shook his head, and said—

"It will soon be all over with her," hearing which Jennie set up a piteous wail, which seemed to rouse the sufferer, for she opened her eyes, looked at her niece, and tried to speak, then sank into unconsciousness again.

Mrs. Walker instantly threw her arm round Jennie, and begged she would strive to keep quiet, for fear of disturbing her aunt. Remedies were sent for and applied, and once Mrs. Storey so far rallied as to smile at Jennie, who kissed her aunt's forehead whilst the hot tears fell upon it. It was a last farewell, for neither ice nor restorative had any power to arrest the departing spirit.

When all was over Jennie gave way to wild fits of grief, reproaching herself bitterly for want of kindness and consideration towards her aunt during the two years and a half they had spent together. The young girl had never seen death before, and the suddenness with which it came made the shock the greater.

She would have to go home after the funeral. In the meantime Mrs. Walker kindly invited Jane to stay with her and her family next door. During these days Jennie found time to take leave of Mrs. Lester and friends in the town. The lady was most kind and sympathising, and Jane was sorry to say good-bye to her. The sad day of the funeral came and went, after which Jane Bowman returned home to her parents and friends.

The shock she had felt made her think. Thoughts of the uncertainty of life were forced upon her. She realised the powerlessness of any one to resist death when the Almighty God calls the spirit hence. Jennie's mind was filled with wonderings as to what was the state of her aunt's soul, it having gone to "the undiscovered country from whose bourn no traveller returns." How empty everything earthly seemed! how great and awful God was! Poor child! she did not then know Him as He is revealed in Christ; but a time was coming when He would be made known to her in His infinite love. She now saw a little, though but a very little, of His majesty and power. Jennie felt as if she could never again be trifling in the house of God, never again laugh over her Bible nor on her knees, as she had often done, nor join in jokes about Bible things, as had formerly been the case with her. Never more would she go about thoughtlessly singing hymns to the words of which her heart could not respond.

Well would it be for us all if we realised more of the greatness of "the Majesty on High," and reverenced more truly the name of God, His Word, His day, His House, and all that points to Him. Angels

F

veil their faces in His presence, as unworthy to
appear in the grandeur of His holiness, "and all the
inhabitants of the earth are reputed as nothing; and
He doeth according to His will in the army of heaven,
and among the inhabitants of the earth; and none
can stay His hand, or say unto Him, What doest
Thou?" (Daniel iv. 35). "God is love," but at the
same time He is "a great God, a mighty, and a
terrible" (Deuteronomy x. 17).

CHAPTER VII.

"It is the secret sympathy,
The silver link, the silken tie,
Which heart to heart, and mind to mind,
In body and in soul can bind."—SCOTT.

"Some chord in unison with what we hear
Is touched within us, and the heart replies."
—COWPER.

IT may be remembered that at Elsie Dale's little working party she was told that Annie Bennett had been taken ill, upon which Elsie determined to call on the sick girl and do her best to make friends with the timid and retiring Annie, a sketch of whose life will here be given at different times.

Annie Bennett was an only child, and but three years old when her mother died. Annie's father had fallen a victim to typhoid fever six months before. Mrs. Bennett's sister, to whom she was much attached, was married to a carpenter living in the sea-side village of Waterend, three miles from Wilminster. Mrs. Sheldon and her husband had no children. He kindly and readily agreed to his

wife's suggestion that they should take the little
Annie and bring her up as their own at her mother's
death, the promise of which helped to cheer the
dying hours of the poor woman.

The Sheldons were kind-hearted people, and became very fond of their young niece; but they did
not understand the wants and wishes of children,
keeping Annie too much apart from others of her
own age. They taught her themselves till they could
do so no longer, and at last sent her to the parish
school; yet even there she had but little intercourse
with her schoolfellows out of lesson time, for Mrs.
Sheldon generally came to fetch her home as soon as
it was over.

Annie's companions thought her old-fashioned,
prim, and consequential. None of them drew to her,
and the poor little girl sometimes felt very lonely.

She was allowed to attend the Sunday-school,
where she had a kind teacher. Annie longed to be
able to talk to her as freely as the rest of the girls in
her class. The lady taught them truths which interested the child, and made her think and wonder;
but then there was no one to whom she could speak
about them

Miss Hastings, her teacher, determined to draw
Annie out, and walked home with her one Sunday,
talked kindly to her, and said that Annie should
come and see her some week-day, which was named,

when she would show the child some things which would both please and surprise her.

Annie made small advances in breaking through her reserve, which cost her some effort, though appearing very little in themselves. She became increasingly fond of Miss Hastings, and began to talk about her and the subjects of interest at home; but no corresponding sympathy was shown there, nor pleasure manifested in them. This was disappointing and discouraging. She soon ceased to attempt to gain the attention of her aunt and uncle with regard to the new ideas which occupied her mind.

As Annie grew up, Mrs. Sheldon taught her as much as circumstances would allow of common work which might prove serviceable to the girl, and made her useful in the house. When a child, Annie had her toys and enjoyed them by herself. Becoming older, she was supplied with a few amusing books; but even these will not always bring cheerfulness and change of thought. A feeling of dulness would often steal over her, and then she would long for companions of her own age. There were one or two whom she met occasionally, but they had not much in common with her.

A thought entered Annie's mind one day, which gradually took possession of her; but she dared not mention it to her aunt or uncle. They had brought her up as their own daughter, and had never intended her to go to service. It would seem as if she were growing tired of their company, or unmindful of their affectionate kindness, if she were but to hint at such a thing. Still the want of interest in life increased. One day, however, when Annie felt a little freer than usual, her secret wish was told without much preparation.

She and her aunt had been sitting at their needle-work by the fire. They had laid aside their stitching for a few minutes' rest, before the little lamp was lighted. Mrs. Sheldon had been talking of something which had occurred when she was a servant at Mossy Grange.

"I shouldn't mind going into service, Aunt Emma."

"Whatever could have put such a fancy into your head, my dear? You don't mean it, I suppose?"

"Well, Auntie, I should like it."

"You silly child! you don't know when you're well off. You'd soon wish yourself back again with your old aunt and uncle. No, no; you must stop and take care of them."

Nothing more was said at the time, but the poor girl felt very disappointed. One day she happened to meet Miss Hastings, her former Sunday-school teacher. The lady stopped to speak to Annie, and asked her if she was thinking of learning to be a servant. Annie said how much she was inclined for it, feeling she was not really wanted at home, and wishing to be of some use in the world, besides longing for companions of her own age, but her aunt and uncle would not hear of such a thing.

Miss Hastings called on Mrs. Sheldon, and asked if she did not think it would be well for Annie to know how to do housework, or to be able to turn her hand to some branch of service, unless Mrs. Sheldon was intending that her niece should learn to be a milliner or dressmaker. At first the idea was strongly opposed, but Miss Hastings led Mrs. Sheldon to see that it would be advisable that she should consent to part with Annie for a time with this object in view. The aunt considered the matter well; but it was several weeks before she could make up her mind to let Annie go.

All was then talked over with uncle James, who saw no necessity for the girl to leave her comfortable home, and was surprised, and a little hurt, on finding it was her own wish. However, he gave in afterwards, saying that women had odd fancies, but he supposed they must be humoured; and perhaps, after all, it wouldn't be a bad plan for the lass to have some line of work in which she could employ herself in case of need. So Mrs. Sheldon began to look out for a suitable situation in Wilminster, and wisely determined not to be hurried in her choice. Annie,

knowing but little of the world, was hardly capable
of judging for herself, besides she could trust her
aunt's judgment. Although beginning to shrink,
not a little, from the idea of being thrown amongst
strangers, Annie remembered it had been her own
wish to become a servant, and she knew she must
abide by it now.

At last there was an opening, and Mrs. Sheldon
and her niece began to make preparation for the
latter to go as under-housemaid in a large estab-
lishment.

When the time came, she was very sorry to leave
her kind aunt and uncle, as they also were to part
with her.

Annie felt strange and homesick in her new place
at first, but the pleasure of having attained what
had seemed so desirable helped her on. She was
also earning her own living, and her days were
more busily and more cheerfully occupied than at
home. She learnt her work well, for " where there's
a will there's a way."

Yet a feeling of disappointment gradually came
over Annie. She had eagerly longed for friends
amongst her fellow-servants, but was slow in making
them, not understanding how to set about that which
most girls find very easy. Being unusually quiet
and reserved, she was in consequence much over-
looked, and but little noticed or thought of by her

companions. Her occasional remarks passed almost unheeded.

After having been in her situation a week or ten days, Annie had the delight of a visit from her aunt, who took a walk with her.

"I keep myself to myself," said the niece, "for nobody here seems to care a straw about me."

Mrs. Sheldon was sorry to find that Annie was disappointed, and felt annoyed with the other servants for being so inconsiderate to her, resolving she should not stay at Mrs. Harding's to be unhappy, and trying to inspirit the girl to carry all off with a high hand.

Annie, however, grew more accustomed to her life, and when she had become better acquainted with her fellow-servants was more cheerful, and did not wish to have the ordeal again of going amongst strangers. Therefore she remained at Mrs. Harding's.

Mrs. Lester having given an invitation to the servants there to join her Bible-class, it was decided for Annie and the kitchen-maid to attend it, which led to a kind of quiet friendship springing up between these girls. The more lively kitchen-maid at first thought Annie "an odd one," as she expressed it, but succeeded in drawing her out a little. Then Annie began to cling to Mary Anne, though the latter was not exactly the friend she had desired. Mary Anne often laughed at her companion for knowing no more than a baby of the ways of the world.

On leaving the class some of the young women would try to make friends with Annie, but she was too reserved, and notwithstanding all their efforts, she kept very much apart from the rest, although Mary Anne was friendly with everybody.

Annie felt proud and unhappy. Still she went regularly, for her mistress expected her to do that. She would never read a text or give an answer if she could possibly help it. However, she gradually became less distant in manner.

One day Mrs. Lester saw her alone and tried to win her confidence, but though apparently pleased and grateful for the interest shown in her, Annie gave no clue whatever to her thoughts and feelings. Mrs. Lester felt discouraged, yet still spoke kindly and encouragingly to the young servant, and directed her to the Best Friend whose love alone could satisfy her heart.

They then knelt in prayer. When they arose from their knees the tears overflowed Annie's eyes. Miss Hastings had been very kind, but no one, not even she, had touched the hidden springs of feeling as Mrs. Lester did that afternoon. A great impression was made on the young girl, much greater than her teacher herself was aware of, for Annie was little accustomed to anything of the sort. She naturally repelled sympathy, and, as a rule, whatever kindness was shown her was usually on the surface; but Mrs. Lester had a power of sympathy which Annie had felt irresistible. She had at first steeled herself against it, yet it had penetrated into her feelings of dulness and loneliness, of longing for love and companionship. It had come like a warm summer wind, and her ice-bound heart melted before the softening breeze. She began to desire the " Friend who sticketh closer than a brother." She was truly grateful to Mrs. Lester for her kindness, but far too shy and reserved to tell her so, and never even thought of making such an effort.

Again and again, for many days, Annie pondered over her teacher's words, and became much more deeply interested in the Bible lessons than she had been before her interview with Mrs. Lester. Still there was no sign of this, as Annie had always appeared attentive at the class.

When she had been about ten months in her situation the poor girl caught cold on her chest, and not taking proper precaution and care, it settled there. She still came to the Bible-class, but all noticed how ill she looked, and her cough was distressing.

As it continued, Mrs. Lester begged her not to come again till it was better, but to keep indoors for a time, and to tell her mistress about it, who would certainly desire this if she knew how far from well her young servant was.

Mrs. Harding was kind. She felt troubled about Annie, and asked her why she had not spoken on the subject before. The lady having a housekeeper saw but little of her younger servants, and as the kitchen and servants' rooms were away from the rest of the house, she had heard nothing of the coughing which had alarmed some in the class.

She found fault with the housekeeper for not informing her of Annie's cough. Mrs. Shipley excused herself by saying she had given the girl a cough mixture to take, and had fully intended to speak to Mrs. Harding about her if she were not better soon. Annie herself had made light of it. The next day being bright, her mistress sent her to a doctor, and Mrs. Shipley accompanied her.

He said that it would not do to trifle with such a cough ; that Annie's lungs were in a delicate state. He would call and speak to Mrs. Harding. In the meantime he gave her some medicine to take with her.

Dr. Barry came in a day or two and told Mrs. Harding that her servant required the greatest care. She was on the verge of consumption. He asked if any of her family were consumptive. On hearing that her mother had died of this complaint he shook his head, and added, " If you follow out my directions, and if you are careful of yourself, I hope you will be better before long; but otherwise, I will not answer for the consequences."

Notwithstanding that Annie was watched over most kindly, and in spite of her own endeavours to carry out the doctor's advice, she became worse instead of better. It was evident that she would have to go home, so her aunt came and took her away when she had been about a year in service.

CHAPTER VIII.

" Actions speak louder than words."

ONE Sunday there appeared at Mrs. Lester's class a taking sort of girl with a very plausible manner. She was attentive, and very quick at answering questions and finding Scripture proofs, but, on leaving, she was disposed to laugh and talk with the most thoughtless.

Margaret Stone, for that was her name, was then seventeen. Her aunt and grandfather, who had brought her up, had instructed her well in the truths of the Bible. The kind old man was a devoted Christian, but he spoilt Margaret, by bringing her too forward, and leading her to express more than she felt on religion. For this she was quite ready, seeing it gratified him, and that he admired her in consequence. Her grandfather thought she was a child of God, and Margaret believed so too, but the reality of her profession had to be proved.

She was pleased to go to Mrs. Lester's when invited to have a little conversation with her, and at first gave the impression of being a decidedly Christian young woman, and one who was likely to be a help in the class; but, on closer converse, the suspicion would recur to her teacher's mind that the girl was talking for effect. She would often drag in a text, or part of a text of Scripture, if it seemed to suit her purpose, without any idea of being a hypocrite, just by way of saying what she considered was the right thing, and what might be expected of her as a Christian. Mrs. Lester, however, fancied she detected a want of reality in her words and manner.

"Margaret," she said, "you make a great profession of religion, but not more than is real, I hope. We must bear in mind our Lord's words, 'By their fruits ye shall know them.' I trust you will prove yourself a true servant of Christ by seeking to know and do God's will in what lies before you. What do you think He expects of you?"

"To be faithful to my mistress."

"Yes, that is part of your duty, and faithfulness includes much. It means honesty, truthfulness, and an earnest fulfilling of the services required of you; but your mistress is not the only one whom you are called to serve for Christ's sake, is she?"

Margaret looked surprised, and said—

"I haven't a master, ma'am, and there are no young ladies nor gentlemen."

"Perhaps not; but I think you said you had two fellow-servants?"

"Yes, ma'am, but I am not under them."

"That may be; but still there is a service of love which the Lord's people should seek to render to all around, especially to those with whom they live, besides their duties to their own relations. Then, too, the servants of the Heavenly Master may not give way to idleness, but they must be willing to help, and ready to deny themselves. This, perhaps, sounds hard, but love to Him will make it easier. Have you ever been in service before?"

"Yes, ma'am, I was at the grocer's in our village for one year. Then the lady at the Hall had me there to take the place of a servant who was ill. I left to go to Mrs. Dixon's. The grocer's people got me a missionary collecting-box, and when I can, I put coppers into it, or get my friends to do so."

"I am glad to hear it. What made you take the box?" said Mrs. Lester, hoping that this was the sign of some good fruit.

"Well, ma'am, you see, they pressed me to take it, and I didn't like to seem unwilling. But, dear me, it'll want a lot to fill it. I must ask for more money. It isn't much I can afford to put in myself, but I tell others it's a privilege to give."

"I hope *you* consider it so, and that you are ready to practise self-denial in little things, in order to have something extra for your box? You may drop that in for me," said Mrs. Lester, giving Margaret a silver coin.

This young woman's life did not correspond with her words. She was idle, careless, and required much looking after. She also fell into some very unpleasant ways, one day being found reading a letter which had been left by her mistress on her dressing-table; and on another occasion she was discovered tying up a parcel, the string of which she had unfastened to look at the purchase contained in the paper. Mrs. Dixon's wardrobe had also undergone inspection several times. Margaret's curiosity increased so that she would pry into everything around that did not concern her. She was not dishonest to begin with, but the untrustworthy habit grew upon her, and from merely *looking at* what did not belong to her, she went on to *covet* the things of others, and at last learned to *take* what was not her own.

After a time the collecting-box was wanted for opening at a missionary meeting, but Margaret had already opened it, and had appropriated the contents. She took no notice of a letter addressed to her asking her to bring or send the box, so one was written to Mrs. Dixon inquiring whether a young person named Margaret Stone was in her service, and stating the reason for the inquiry. In this way the girl's con-

G

duct with regard to the box became known, and all her efforts to conceal the truth and excuse herself were in vain.

"I could not have supposed this of you, Margaret," her mistress said. "It is bad enough to rob our fellow-creatures, but think of the sin of robbing God! You have received money from others to send the gospel to the heathen; this is God's work; and the money which has been given to Him for this purpose, you have spent upon yourself! How much did you take out? Tell me honestly. Do not attempt to keep back a part. Remember Ananias and Sapphira." *

"There was eight-and-sevenpence in."

"Then I shall withhold that from your wages, and send it to the missionary collector. Have you ever taken anything else that did not belong to you, since you have been in my service? All shall be forgiven now, if you will frankly acknowledge it, and if you will promise me that you will seek God's help to be strictly honest in the future."

Margaret owned to several acts of dishonesty in little things. Her mistress spoke so kindly to her, whilst she pointed out the sin of such conduct, and was at the same time so forgiving, that the girl's heart was melted, and she felt ashamed and sorry for what she had done.

* Acts v. 1-10.

"You must confess your guilt to God with regard to all you have told me, and ask pardon of Him for His dear Son's sake," Mrs. Dixon added.

Margaret did seem penitent, and her mistress soon saw a marked change for the better in many ways, and endeavoured to encourage her in what was right. Mrs. Dixon observed that she was much more humble in manner, and more guarded in what she said, and therefore learnt to trust her as she had never done before.

Several months passed by. A niece of Mrs. Dixon's was staying with her. They were sitting together conversing over their work.

"That is a good girl," Miss Harris said to her aunt, speaking of Margaret. "I've noticed in many little particulars that she *acts* the Christian. When I was here before, if you gave her an opportunity, she would talk to any amount in a religious strain, but what unpleasant ways she had! Margaret certainly did not practise what she preached; but now it is just the contrary. She says less, but lives more up to the profession she makes."

"I am very glad to hear you say so, Ellen," was the reply, "and I quite agree with you. 'Actions speak louder than words.' The girl has been different ever since that affair of the missionary box."

The evening before Miss Harris left, Mrs. Dixon had given an entertainment to a party of friends.

After her niece's departure the next morning, she employed herself by counting over the plate. To her dismay a dessert-spoon was missing. Margaret assured her that she had brought up all the silver. Her fellow-servants knew nothing about it. Every likely place was searched again and again, but the spoon was not forthcoming. The servants went about with melancholy faces. Their spare time was spent in looking for it, and in racking their brains to think of some hitherto unthought-of way in which the spoon might have disappeared.

Mrs. Dixon was perplexed. She could not doubt the honesty of the two servants who had been with her for many years, and she felt most unwilling to charge Margaret with having taken it. When asked, she denied all knowledge of it, though her eyes were often red with crying. Day after day went by, and she looked pale and ill.

"I will not doubt the poor girl's word," her kind mistress said to herself. "She is not what she used to be, and her manner now gives me confidence. I have trusted her of late, and I can and will trust her still, notwithstanding appearances being all against her. The Lord can, and I feel sure He will, make known the truth in this mysterious matter, in answer to prayer;" and something to the same effect she said to Margaret.

It occurred to Mrs. Dixon to write and tell Miss

Harris about the trouble, as possibly she might suggest an idea which would throw light upon the subject. This answer came by return of post :—

"MY DEAR AUNT,—I am so sorry for your difficulty, and have been turning over in my mind every trifle that has happened lately; but I fear I cannot help you in this most unpleasant business. I can recall nothing in which a spoon bore a part, except, indeed, when spoons in general were required, the night before I left you.

"As Margaret has been dishonest, though not for some time past, I cannot help suspecting her. Shall you have her boxes searched? The old temptation may have come over her again, and she would then most likely continue to deny having taken it. I do not like to say, or even to think this, as she has so much improved. I wish, with all my heart, it may not be the case. In haste.—Believe me, your affectionate niece,   JULIA HARRIS.

"*P.S.*—By-the-bye, since writing this, I have remembered that Mrs. Stock had some arrow-root made for her. I have a dim recollection of stirring it with a dessert-spoon before the child took it away. Have you asked the old woman about it?"

Here was a ray of hope.

"I will go myself to Mrs. Stock's."

And Mrs. Dixon went immediately. After answering the lady's kind inquiries as to her health, the poor old woman said—

"Ah! my dear lady, I be right glad to see ye; and thank ye for what ye sent me. I've had the basin ready to go back, and the spoon along with it, when I could get a body to take it; but little Molly hasn't been up here sin' she fetched the arrerroot. And the girl as does for me is allus in a hurry-scurry; but I've kept the spoon wrapted up in paper agin any one should look in."

The relief and joy that this discovery brought was great. How thankful Mrs. Dixon felt that she had continued to trust Margaret through all this perplexity! How overjoyed the poor girl was to know that there was no longer cause for suspecting her! How happy the other servants were that all was right again!

Margaret felt she could never be grateful enough for the confidence her mistress had placed in her who had formerly been dishonest, and for having been allowed to remain in the service of Mrs. Dixon, to whom she became devotedly attached. Though making less religious profession than she had done five or six months before, it was proved to be genuine by all her outward conduct, for "*actions speak louder than words.*"

CHAPTER IX.

"Beauty is truth, truth beauty."—J. KEATS.

"For Truth has such a face and such a mien
As to be loved needs only to be seen."—DRYDEN.

> " *Transparent* as the crystal spring,
>   Which ripples from the mountain's crest ;
> *Clear* as the song-bird's carolling,
>   To list'ning mate in night's still rest ;
> *Unsullied* as the morning dews,
>   Or sparkling snow on Alpine height,
> *Telling high birth* as sunset'hues
>   Bear glowing witness to the light ;
> So glorious is heav'n-born Truth, so nobly fair,
> *Dauntless* and *valiant* all her sons, *free* as the moun-
>   tain air.

AFTER Caroline Hall's illness, her father wished her
to remain at home for a time, to regain her strength
before taking another situation. She helped her
stepmother, and took in a little needlework as soon
as she was able. She had been at Selbridge eight
or nine months, was then about twenty years of age,
and had much improved in appearance and manners.
Caroline was fond of her country home, which was
always beautifully clean and nice. On an old-

fashioned secretary she had arranged some pretty flowers in quaint vases, as well as on the window-sill; for she was in the habit of making the kitchen look bright and cheerful in this way. The old clock in the large wooden case had just struck four this sunny afternoon of which I am about to speak, when a carriage stopped at the garden gate. A gentleman and lady alighted, and walked up the path towards the cottage.

"Does Mr. Hall—Edmund Hall, the blacksmith —live here?" the gentleman asked.

"He does, sir; and if you will please to step in, I will go and fetch him," said Mrs. Hall.

They entered, and took the chairs she placed for them, whilst she hastened to tell her husband, wondering why he could be wanted by these stranger gentlefolks. Caroline had gone over to see Mattie.

Whilst Mr. and Mrs. Ashton, for that was their name, are waiting till the blacksmith has made him-self look somewhat more presentable, it will be well to explain the cause of their visit.

Mr. Ashton was brother to Edmund Hall's first wife, and was abroad when their mother died. The bulk of her property had sunk with her, and what should have come to her daughter was grossly mis-managed, and poor Miss Ashton was left in extreme poverty. After a while she heard that the situation

of parish schoolmistress at Selbridge was vacant.
She sought and obtained it. Edmund Hall lived in
the village, and was a steady young man, well-to-do
in his line of life. He was kind-hearted and pleasant
in manner. Hall much admired the young schoolmistress, whom he greatly pitied for the loss she had
sustained in the death of her mother, and on account
of her altered circumstances. He aimed at showing
her such kindness and attention as lay in his power;
and, after a time, a mutual attachment was formed,
which ended in their marriage. During her married
life, which only lasted four years, Mrs. Hall had but
little correspondence with her brother, who had
settled in Canada. She had informed him of the
birth of her baby; and, later on, her husband had
written in deep distress, telling Mr. Ashton of his
wife's death of consumption, when the child was
between two and three years of age.

Mr. Ashton married and became a prosperous
man. After many years he returned to England
with his wife, and brought his two sons to place them
at college.

He had long wished to learn particulars of the
daughter his poor sister had left, and he and Mrs.
Ashton had just taken the first opportunity of going
to Selbridge to make inquiries.

It was an exciting visit to Caroline's father, who
promised she should shortly spend a week with her

aunt and uncle in London, where Mr. Ashton had taken a furnished house for a few months.

The lady and gentleman were pleased with the honest blacksmith, who was a good-looking man of about five-and-forty years; and he and his wife, in their turn, thought their visitors "most pleasant-spoken people," whilst Hall was much gratified by their kind thought of his daughter, and Mr. Ashton's remembrance of her mother, which was deeply affectionate after an absence of twenty-five years.

"Fine hearing for Caroline when she comes back!" exclaimed her father after he and his wife had seen Mr. and Mrs. Ashton drive away in the carriage.

"Well, it is to be sure!" said Mrs. Hall. "Who'd have dreamed of such a thing? Wonders never cease!"

They had scarcely finished their tea when Caroline appeared.

"A piece of news for you, Carrie! Guess who we've had here," said her father, with a merry twinkle in his eyes.

After several wrong shots she gave it up.

"Well, you'll never hit the mark, so I'll tell you," he said.

Caroline was indeed astonished to hear of all that had passed, and of the visit in prospect for her. Poor girl! it was almost enough to turn her head, what with the pleasure and excitement it caused, combined with many nervous fears.

The eagerly anticipated, but also much dreaded, time arrived. Caroline had done her best to make herself look neat and respectable, and her father had given her a present in money to help her. Her step-mother had also been kind in working for her.

Hall travelled with his daughter a short distance, saw her into the train for London, and then returned home. On entering the bustling London station, her heart beat very fast, she was so unaccustomed to travelling. Her uncle had, however, promised to meet her, and Mrs. Ashton had previously sent a blue necktie, by wearing which Caroline might be identified. She stepped out of the railway carriage on to the crowded platform, and vainly endeavoured to discover her insignificant little box from amongst the huge quantity of luggage. At last, to her great relief, it was taken out of the van. Looking anxious and heated, she gazed timidly round at the ladies and gentlemen as they moved rapidly away. After all, she had not waited long when her uncle came forward, inquired, "Is this my niece, Caroline Hall?" and shook hands with her on finding he was right in his conjecture. He was a gentlemanly man, apparently about fifty years of age. He soon set Caroline at ease, and they left the station in a cab.

Mr. Ashton made kind inquiries about her parents,

the improvement in her health since the illness, her
past history, and other subjects of interest. He drew
his niece out in conversation in so cheerful and
pleasant a manner, that she was almost ready to
forget her fears and anxieties respecting the aunt
she had not yet seen, when, after a drive of half-an-
hour, the cab stopped at a nice house, small compared with that in which her aunt and uncle were
accustomed to live, but formidably grand to the poor
young daughter of the Selbridge blacksmith. She
was relieved to see a maid-servant come to the door,
and not a footman in livery.

Mrs. Ashton quickly made her appearance, and
kindly welcomed the trembling girl, who was blush-
ing almost to tears.

"Come into the dining-room, Caroline, and warm
yourself by the fire, before you take off your things,"
said her aunt, leading her into the room. "You
must want your dinner. We are going to dine
earlier to-day. Now we wish you to make yourself
quite at home," added the lady, seeing the painfully
shy look on her niece's face.

"Thank you, ma'am," she whispered.

"No, no; you must not call me 'ma'am'; you
must call me 'Aunt Louisa.'"

After a few minutes of friendly talk, Mrs. Ashton
took Caroline to the room where she was to sleep,
and left her to make herself neat, saying, "Dinner

will be ready as soon as you are, dear. The drawing-room is just across the passage; but perhaps, as you know the way, you would prefer coming into the dining-room at once. Ring your bell if you want anything, Charlotte will come."

"Oh, thank you," Caroline replied, in a low tone. "I think I can find my way to the dining-room." She dared not say "ma'am" again, and had not the courage to address Mrs. Ashton as "Aunt Louisa."

It was a relief to be left alone, if only for a few minutes. She could have sat down and cried, feeling everything so grand and unlike home, and having a terrible fear of saying or doing what might seem unmannerly to her aunt and uncle, or what would reveal to the servants the humble station in which she had been brought up.

She was not long in going downstairs; her aunt hastened from the drawing-room to join her, on hearing her footsteps.

Both Mr. and Mrs. Ashton were most kind and hospitable, but how much Caroline wished she could have dined with the servants! However, by degrees, she became less diffident.

When she went to her room that night, her aunt accompanied her to see that she wanted nothing, and said cheerfully, "Now Caroline, my dear, you must try and make yourself at home with us. Your uncle and I shall like it so much better. I can quite understand your feeling shy at first, not having been accustomed to our way of life; but you will soon be used to it."

"Oh, you're so very kind, Aunt Louisa!" Caroline managed to say, colouring up; "I'm sure I ought to feel at home; but I don't wish to disgrace you."

"Nonsense, nonsense, you silly little woman!" said Mrs. Ashton merrily. "Do not be afraid, my child, or else you will not enjoy your visit, and that would be a pity. Your uncle and I will make excuses, if necessary. Never think about the servants. If *we* do not mind, surely *you* need not trouble yourself."

Caroline thanked her aunt gratefully, and was cheered. She soon became more at ease. Her uncle took her to see the sights of London; and she did enjoy herself very much.

The day she returned to Selbridge, when she was preparing for her departure, Mr. and Mrs. Ashton were in the drawing-room together.

"What do you think of Caroline?" asked her uncle.

"I consider her a very nice girl," was the reply. "She is overcoming her extreme shyness, and is coming out brightly. I think she has some very good qualities, and that she is naturally refined."

"Yes; and naturally timid too, I should say."

"Well, yes; but we cannot wonder at her feeling awkward and uncomfortable at first, being taken, as she was, from her humble position to be a lady, all at once, and that amongst strangers, though relatives," said her aunt.

"No, indeed; poor child! I like the simplicity and truthfulness I see in her."

"Yes; that is, to my mind, the chief beauty of her character, as far as I know of her at present. I have often noticed how careful Caroline is to speak the truth, and to avoid giving a false impression."

"She reminds me of her poor dear mother, so delicate and refined in appearance," said Mr. Ashton with a sigh.

"Oh, she is a sweet-looking girl, and her manners are ladylike for the sphere in which she has been brought up!"

Well was it for Caroline that she had learnt to be truthful, and that, too, from the best motive!

Her uncle went with her to the station, and saw her off. He and her aunt had made her beautiful presents, in books and other things.

The change had been beneficial to Caroline's health and spirits. She was, however, sometimes a little unsettled by it, and inclined to wish that her circumstances were different; but she did not yield to discontented feelings. How much she had to tell her parents, and Matilda!

In a few weeks' time the post brought two letters from Mr. Ashton, one addressed to Caroline's father, the other to herself, which was to this effect :—

"MY DEAR NIECE,—I want you to consider well a proposal I am going to make.

"We were pleased with what we saw of you during your visit to us, and think that we might be very happy together. Therefore I am writing to ask if you will come and make our house your home. Your aunt and I will provide for you, and you will be to us as a daughter. I am aware that you are at present uneducated for this position, but you shall have lessons from good teachers in some acquirements, and have other advantages also; whilst your aunt and I will do what we can to help you on in ordinary knowledge.

"Not wishing to take you away without your father's consent, I have written to him on the subject; and I desire that you will talk it all over together. As the child of my dear sister, I am much interested for you, and shall rejoice to promote your welfare.

"We purpose remaining in England till the end of August; and shall want you to spend a month with us a little nearer the time.

"You will, of course, feel leaving your father and friends, but we think you will like Canada, and that you will gain much, if you can make up your mind to fall in with our plan, and forsake the Old World for the New.

"Your Aunt joins me in love, and in hoping that you will accede to our wishes, so that we may welcome you as a daughter to our Canadian home.—Your affectionate uncle,   SAMUEL ASHTON.

"Do not be longer than a week in replying to this."

It was indeed a great surprise, to both Caroline and her father, to receive the letters from Mr. Ashton. They could not be otherwise than much gratified by his kindness. Poor Caroline was almost bewildered with excitement at first. It would be such a great change to her to become a lady! and then to go to Canada! but she did not like the thought of leaving her father, and was glad to have a few days in which to weigh the matter carefully. He and all her friends wished her to accept the offer, which, they said, would be the making of her.

As there seemed nothing to prevent, but every reason why she should take this step,—after much prayer for guidance, she wrote gratefully, agreeing to the plan. This being done, the prospect seemed to brighten, notwithstanding the shrinking Caroline still felt at going so far away from her father and friends.

During the month she spent in London she was

H

taken to see much that was new and most wonderful to her; also to purchase suitable clothing. Afterwards she returned to Selbridge to say good-bye.

Matilda came to spend a day with her at her father's house before she left England. Many bitter tears were shed at the parting between the girls. Mr. and Mrs. Ashton, always kind and considerate, had provided their niece with pocket money to make her parents and friends presents on leaving.

She and her stepmother took a more loving farewell of each other than would have seemed possible a year or more before. The day Caroline left Selbridge her father accompanied her to London, and remained till the next morning to see the last of her as the vessel sailed from the docks. They both felt the parting very much. He missed her sadly at first; and so did Mattie.

Arriving in Canada, all was new and delightful to Caroline. She applied herself very diligently to her studies; and, after a little time, became fairly acquainted with them. She learnt much by observation and by inquiry of her aunt and uncle; and they taught her many things. In the meanwhile, she was quite a companion and a real comfort to them, as might be expected from her affectionate and clinging nature, and by reason of the gratitude their kindness called forth.

After three or four years she was married suitably

to her new position. Her husband had been previously informed of her history; he was well calculated to promote her happiness, especially in the best way of all.

But, it may be asked, what of good, bright Mattie? Though her path in life was less brilliant than her friend's, perhaps it was equally happy. Both were useful in different ways, and sought to live for God and those around them.

Matilda was married when about four-and-twenty, and she could not have made a better choice. John Harvey was older than herself. He had saved sufficient money to stock a small shop; but difficulties in trade so reduced their means, that they were thankful to emigrate to Canada, on the promise of Caroline's husband to give them a start in business there. Thus Matilda went to live near her former friend, which was a great pleasure to both; and Caroline was able to return the kindness shown to her by Matilda in days of trouble and sickness.

We must now wish them farewell, and leave them in the misty distance of a land beyond our horizon.

CHAPTER X.

"Stand up ! stand up for Jesus !
　Stand in His strength alone ;
The arm of flesh will fail you—
　Ye dare not trust your own :
Put on the Gospel armour,
　And watching unto prayer,
Where duty calls, or danger,
　Be never wanting there."—G. DUFFIELD.

ON Annie Bennett's return home, Mrs. Sheldon and her husband were grieved to see the change in her, and wished she had never left them. They had known of her being out of health, and her aunt had been once or twice to see her, and had wanted her to go back with her; but, each time, the poor girl thought she should soon be better, and therefore felt it would not be wise to give up her place. The alteration in her for the worse had been great since her aunt's last visit to her.

For two or three weeks after her return, Annie came downstairs about eleven o'clock in the morning; then not till dinner time. Presently she could not leave her room till the afternoon; and, later on, only for an hour and a half in the evening. At last even that became too great an effort, although her uncle brought her down, and carried her up in his arms at night.

Mrs. Lester occasionally called to see Annie, but little guessed, from the sick girl's reserved manner, how much these opportunities were enjoyed, nor how deeply she entered into the reading and exposition of Scripture.

There were some in the Bible class who had become very anxious about their former companion, for they knew the importance of insuring an interest in Christ, and longed to know the state of her soul. Though led to hope the best from her attention at the class, they wanted further evidence than this that she had been born again. She had said nothing, either to Mrs. Lester or to themselves, which would give them ground for confidence respecting her eternal safety.

Elsie Dale wrote to Annie, and both Elsie and Mary Smith went now and then to see her; but they failed to draw her out in conversation; indeed those who were desirous for her spiritual welfare heard nothing, from any quarter, to satisfy their earnest hopes and longings. There was one thing, however, which they could do, and this they did not neglect, and it was to pray for Annie. She was neither forgotten in private intercession, nor at the little meetings of the prayer-union in connection with the Bible-class, which were held weekly.

As it afterwards became known, she had already decided for Christ. He had taken possession of her heart before her illness came on; but she had hitherto spoken to no one of her newly-found peace and joy.

It was true Annie looked happier, that she was very patient in her weakness and suffering, and was often reading her Bible. At first she had shrunk from being seen with it, but gradually the "fear of man" gave way to the eager desire for the "sincere milk of the Word."

Her aunt supposed that such a good-living girl as her niece had always been must be fit to die. How could it be otherwise? Yet Mrs. Sheldon could not account for it—perhaps it was the far-off echo of some sermon she had heard—but the idea haunted her at times, "Supposing Annie should *not* be prepared for death!" Then Mrs. Sheldon would try to shake off the thought, and blame herself for imagining anything so unkind and unreasonable. Still it would return. She had never spoken to Annie with regard to her hope of salvation, but had prided herself on her humility in not venturing to talk about subjects of which she knew almost nothing. Notwithstanding this felt ignorance, neither she nor her husband had sought to know more, either for their own sakes, or for the sake of the precious soul of the niece God had entrusted to their care. To speak *now* to Annie on religion Mrs. Sheldon found to be a very difficult thing.

However, one day, after thinking a long time, she said—

"Annie, my dear, are you happy?"

"Yes, Auntie, thank you; quite happy."

There was a long pause after this. The poor girl was feeling she ought to speak out and tell her aunt the cause of her happiness; but the effort to do so seemed very great. She did not know how to make it. Mrs. Sheldon had never encouraged any religious conversation, in her mistaken view, believing that sacred things were best kept to oneself.

One sentence after another was pondered over by Annie, but just as she was going to speak it died away, or something happened which appeared to make it impossible for her to say what she wished. Why did she not ask to be guided what words to use? And why did she not pray for strength to confess Christ?

Annie was not satisfied to make no confession of Him, and had felt uncomfortable about her silence on that point for a long time past. She saw more and more clearly how ungrateful it was not to acknowledge the Saviour whom she loved and desired to honour; but it was not an easy thing to make a beginning, with a nature so reserved as hers.

At last her aunt spoke again.

"If you were to die, my dear—not that I mean to say you *are* going to leave us, pray don't think that —but—well," she hesitated, "where would you go?"

"To heaven, Aunt Emma." She prayed for help, and then added, "For Jesus Christ's sake."

This was a commencement. It was pressing the thin end of the wedge under the great difficulty. Mrs. Sheldon kissed her niece, and felt assured that she was ready for her change. Annie was happier for having made this little effort in the right direction.

Life seemed fast ebbing away with her. She could not but fear that her aunt and uncle were unprepared to meet her above. She wished to speak to them personally on the subject, before the opportunity should have passed for ever; and for many days she prayed to be enabled to do so. Annie often asked one or the other to read to her out of the Bible, hoping that the chapters she chose would come home to them.

The conviction weighed upon her mind that she had not confessed Christ in her time of health and strength, after He had made Himself known to her as her Saviour; that she had not witnessed for Him;

that she had given no testimony to her loving Lord.

Annie was desirous to honour Him, late though it was, by letting her Bible-class companions know the change that had taken place in her thoughts and feelings since she first appeared amongst them. It might be that a few words from their dying friend would help them to come to Jesus, or encourage them to trust Him more entirely. She would like her kind teacher to be told that it was she, with God's blessing, who had first led her, the close, reserved servant-girl, to long truly to have the Lord Jesus Christ as her Best Friend.

Though anxious to know Annie's state of mind, Mrs. Lester had left off asking her questions, finding it useless, and that it only seemed to make matters worse. When she came, she read and talked gently to the invalid, and prayed with her. Friends had for long, in private, besought the Lord that Annie might be enabled to open her heart to those who were spiritually interested for her, and who might be made the means of blessing to her.

It was ten days since Mrs. Lester had called. She had been prevented from paying her weekly visit at Waterend. The morning, in August, of which I am about to speak, Annie had been much in prayer that the Lord Jesus would give her grace to confess Him, and she felt strengthened, believing He would answer her petitions, and that He would not only enable her to acknowledge Him, but show her how, and lead the way.

She was peacefully resting on the beautiful words of Isaiah xli. 10, "Fear thou not; for I am with thee: be not dismayed; for I am thy God: I will strengthen thee; yea, I will help thee; yea, I will uphold thee with the right hand of My righteousness," when her aunt opened the door, saying—

"Mrs. Lester has come to see you, my dear," and the lady was shown in.

"Take a seat, ma'am, please," said Mrs. Sheldon, dusting a chair with her apron, and then leaving the room.

Having answered Mrs. Lester's kind inquiries about her health, Annie felt it necessary to begin at once to say what she wanted to make known, remembering how dangerous delays had proved to be. The first thing that occurred to her was to speak of the text in Isaiah, as having been such a comfort to her. She looked it out in her Bible, which she handed to Mrs. Lester.

"Yes," was the reply, "that is indeed a beautiful text. I am so glad it has cheered and helped you."

"Mrs. Lester," the sick girl said, with a trembling voice, "I'm happy now. I'm not afraid to die."

The effort to say this had brought the tears to her eyes and the colour to her pale cheeks, but a smile of restful joy lighted up her face.

Taking her hand, Mrs. Lester exclaimed—

"Dear Annie! I am thankful to hear this! How long is it since you found peace?"

"Some months back now, ma'am, or it may be getting on for a year ago. Do you remember talking to me the first time alone, when you told me what a friend I might have in Jesus, if I would look to Him?" she asked with quivering lips.

"Yes, quite well."

The ice had been broken, and Annie continued—

"Well, ma'am, nobody had ever spoken to me so fully and plainly before; and I thought a great deal upon what you said. Day after day I called to mind your words, and I felt how much I needed such a Friend as the Lord Jesus."

She paused for breath, then gathering fresh courage, which increased as she went on with her narration, proceeded—"I was too proud at first to seek pardon through Christ, and so, of course, I could not know Him as my Friend. But one Sunday I heard Mr. Armitage preach from the text, 'A Friend of publicans and sinners,' and I seemed to see myself, oh, such a sinner! though I had always been brought up to be respectable-like."

A fit of coughing interrupted her; but presently she added, "I went back from church as quickly as I could, and reached Mrs. Harding's before the other servants had returned, and those who had not gone out were below, so I had my bedroom free to myself. I locked the door, and on my knees I sought and found the 'Friend of publicans and sinners.'"

Tears stood in Mrs. Lester's eyes.

"Thank God!" were the first words that came to her lips, as soon as she could trust herself to speak. Then she exclaimed, "How glad I and some of your friends in the Bible-class would have been to have known this before!"

And taking Annie's hand she pressed it between both of hers.

"I wish I'd told you when you asked me," said the sick girl with a sigh.

"The Lord Jesus is strengthening you to confess Him now before He takes you home. It must have been a great effort, Annie, to say so much. I hope you will rest quietly for the next two or three hours at least."

Seeing how weary the invalid looked, Mrs. Lester only stayed to offer up a short prayer and thanksgiving, and then asked Mrs. Sheldon, "Will you let your niece have some of the jelly I have brought with me? It is nourishing, and she may be able to sleep after it, which will be the best thing possible just now."

"Yes, ma'am, to be sure I will. You're very good. I shall leave her to herself when she's had it."

Annie lay exhausted indeed, but very happy. She had broken through her barrier of reserve, so far as

Mrs. Lester was concerned, and felt she had her full sympathy; that they were one. Henceforth it would be less difficult to speak out to her teacher, and having been enabled to conquer in this quarter, courage had been gained for further victory.

Annie determined to send a letter to the members of the Bible-class. She only saw one or another now and then, but she could write to all at once. Thinking her strength enough for this, and feeling refreshed by sleep, she asked her aunt for her writing-desk. The letter was begun, but the excitement of composing it was too much for her at that time, and she was soon obliged to leave off. It was, however, finished in a few days, being written at intervals. Perhaps some may be interested in reading

ANNIE'S LETTER.

" DEAR FRIENDS,—You have been so good in asking after me, and sending me nosegays of sweet flowers, or little things to tempt my appetite, that I wish to take up my pen and thank you kindly for them and for all your goodness to me. I'm free to confess that this is not my only reason for writing. I have another, which makes me anxious to write whilst I have enough strength left.

" I want you to know that I'm not afraid to die, because I've come to the Lord Jesus as a poor lost sinner, and have found Him my Saviour and my

Friend. He has 'washed' me from my sins 'in His own blood,' and now I'm quite happy. I wish to tell you this before I die that you may be easy about me, and that those of you who have never taken God's great Gift of a Saviour, and given your hearts to Him, may be helped on to do so. Also I desire to seize this opportunity of confessing Christ before it is too late. I am very sorry I did not honour the Lord with my words in my health and strength. If I were to have that time over again I hope and believe I should be different, but now it is 'better late than never.' The past is forgiven. As to what's to come, I want you all to meet me in heaven. Mind that no one of you is missing there. Jesus Christ is full of love, and waiting to save you as He has saved me. Oh! let Him do it. Perhaps these few poor lines, written by your dying companion, will not be in vain. May God bless you; and may we all, with our dear teacher, and Mr. Armitage and those we love, meet again to part no more.—Your affectionate friend,   ANNIE BENNETT."

The letter was enclosed in a little note to Mrs. Lester, in which Annie requested her to read it to the class the following Sunday. There were many who could not restrain their tears at hearing it, and poor Mrs. Lester could hardly accomplish her task of reading it aloud.

Then, after a short pause, she remarked how thankful and how greatly relieved, she felt sure, many of them would be, as she was, to learn of the happy change which had taken place in Annie Bennett. Mrs. Lester also expressed her fervent desire that those in her class who were still unsaved would solemnly consider the earnest words of their dying friend; and she sincerely hoped that the letter, written by a hand that would soon be stiff in death, might not be without its effect, but that Annie might have the joy of knowing that she had been the means of bringing one sinner, at least, to the Saviour in penitence and faith.

"Some of you have never seen her," Mrs. Lester added; "yet she speaks to you too, and says, 'I want you *all* to meet me in heaven. Mind that no one of you is missing there. Jesus Christ is full of love, and waiting to save you as He has saved me. Oh! let Him do it.'"

All left the class much solemnised after the closing prayer, in which, as usual, requests were offered up for Annie, but this time praise and thanksgiving also ascended on her behalf.

CHAPTER XI.

"Know that pride,
Howe'er disguised in its own majesty,
Is littleness."   —WORDSWORTH.

PERHAPS my readers may recollect that, at the little working-party at Elsie Dale's, allusion was made to Lady Dalby's maid, and that she appeared to be no favourite with some of the girls present there. It is of her I am about to write; but to do so it will be necessary to look back to a rather earlier date than that of the missionary gathering of a few of Elsie's Bible-class companions.

There had been a sharp frost during the night, and although the sun had done his best in the middle of the day to melt the frozen dew, it was freezing again, and many a leaf held its tiny white crystals, and the shady side of the trees in Mr. Nixon's garden still retained the beautiful frosting; but though cold outside, the fire indoors burnt brightly this autumn afternoon, and the ruddy light danced upon portraits of the Nixon family of past generations which hung upon the walls of the drawing-room where Mr.

and Mrs. Nixon, an elderly couple, were seated, looking rather disturbed in mind.

After a pause in their conversation, the doctor said—

"Servants are not what they used to be when we were young. Now they are always chopping and changing, and trying to 'better themselves,' as they call it. Years gone by, they never thought of leaving a good place, unless it were to marry, or unless some unavoidable reason compelled them to take such a step."

"You are quite right, doctor," was the reply.

"I wish they would take a leaf out of their grandmothers' books in this particular. I can call to mind dear old Betty, who lived in my mother's service nearly half-a-century, and then, as she was growing infirm, she was placed in the almshouse, where she spent ten peaceful years before going to her heavenly home. You remember her, William, do you not?" asked the old lady, with a playful pat on his arm.

"To be sure I do, my dear," said her husband. "She was a picture of a servant; so clean and neat; and whilst respectful in manner, at the same time so cheery and kind."

"Ay; and Betty was one of scores of others."

"True. They sometimes remained many years in a situation, becoming strongly attached to, and interested in, all that concerned the family whom they

I

served with devoted affection. I recollect the nurse who took charge of us when we were youngsters," said the doctor.- "Poor old soul! she seemed to think there were no such children in the world; and as for her master and mistress, no others ever could come up to them! It would have broken Jane's heart to leave us when we were little. However, at last we no longer needed her, and she became nurse to a friend of my mother's; but it was a bitter grief to Jane to part from us. My parents would have kept her about them still if they could have afforded it. We never forgot the good woman."

"Faithful servants became a necessary part of the household," said Mrs. Nixon. "They had their faults, no doubt, such as Jane's spoiling you, my dear," she added, with a merry twinkle in her soft brown eyes; "but what honest, industrious creatures they were!"

"Ay; and did not they rise in the morning, to go through with the work of the day, at what would now be considered an unconscionable hour?"

"Yes, indeed! how amazed the present generation would be if they could have a peep at a day in service some fifty years ago!"

"When I was a young practitioner," said Mr. Nixon, "I well remember the kindness and attention with which the old servants nursed any member of the family in sickness, showing themselves, in many instances, very unselfish."

"Yes; and such loyal domestics were justly respected, beloved, and cared for. Even when compelled to leave their places, their wants were still thought of."

"Oh! to be sure! At death the graves of these good people were near, perhaps *in*, the family vault. I can recal several cases in point. At any rate, these faithful servants lived long in the memory of the rising generation."

After a pause the old lady said—

"I have been thinking, dear, how the valuable persons of whom we have been speaking picture to us the higher service of a Heavenly Master."

"You are right, my dear; but go on, I like to hear you."

Nrs. Nixon continued. "Dwelling with Him day by day, do not His interests become more and more the interests of His people? Are they not increasingly taken up with them, so that their own concerns become less to them?"

The worthy couple then went on to say how Christians should learn a lesson from the servants of former years, with regard to serving the Lord Jesus; how such service should be constant, true-hearted, self-sacrificing. As faithful servants would uphold the honour of the masters and mistresses they loved and respected, and would be willing to help any who belonged to them, so the followers of the Lord Jesus should be ready to stand up for the honour of His name against all opposition, and should be glad to show their affection to Him by helping any member of His family.

Perhaps Mr. and Mrs. Nixon made too great a distinction between the servants of days gone by and those of the present time. *All* were not what they ought to have been fifty or seventy years ago; and noble-hearted girls and women may *still* be found in service, who are humbly and earnestly seeking to do their duty in that state of life unto which God has been pleased to call them. Some of these might well compare with the bright examples of a bygone age. Mr. and Mrs. Nixon had, however, been disappointed, and they beheld the existing race of servants through "green spectacles."

The cause of their disappointment was this: Lucy Willington was an upper servant, partly parlour and partly lady's-maid to Mrs. Nixon, to whom she had given notice to leave half-an-hour before the conversation began, and just previous to Mr. Nixon's return, on his grey horse, from visiting the few patients he still attended.

Lucy had only been at Ivy Lodge two months, and her master and mistress felt aggrieved at her conduct. They took a most kindly interest in their servants. Many mistresses would have said, "If she wishes to leave, I am not the one to keep her; let her go, by all means;" but Mrs. Nixon had sincerely sympathised with Lucy in her troubles, and had endeavoured to do as much as possible to comfort and help her. At the same time, the young woman could not have had a nicer situation; and now, for her to give notice to her mistress in some such words as these—"If you please, ma'am, I wish to leave you this day month," was as trying as it was unexpected.

On hearing this, Mrs. Nixon exclaimed, "Indeed, Lucy! What is the reason?"

"Well, ma'am," was the reply, "I feel I'm not treated by your other servants with that respect to which I am entitled."

"What do you mean?"

"They speak and behave to me as if I had never seen better days, and when I tell them of this they are offended, and call me haughty; I can plainly see that we shall never get on together."

"O Lucy! how foolish to throw up a comfortable place for such a reason! Try to pocket your pride, or rather to ask God to subdue it. Though you have been in a higher position, you are but a servant now; therefore endeavour to accommodate yourself to your present circumstances. The girls mean no harm. Determine not to take offence in future, and reconsider the matter. I will speak to them about it, and will give you till to-morrow morning to think it over."

"No, ma'am, thank you; I have made up my mind."

"I am disappointed, Lucy. Your master and I have felt for you. It has been our desire to help you, and we have wished that you should be as happy here as possible. It is not everybody who would be so considerate, nor would every one know what you went through before leaving home."

Mrs. Nixon paused. Lucy was perhaps too proud just then to feel grateful, or, at any rate, to express her gratitude; so she only walked out of the room with a haughty toss of her head, and with an air of offended dignity.

She was a tall, fine-looking young woman, of two-and-twenty years. Her father had been a hairdresser at Wilminster; he was successful in his business for a length of time, and gave his daughters and son a very good education for their position in life. Lucy had refined tastes. She was passionately fond of music, and could sing and play well, considering that her musical advantages had not been great. She was having lessons on the organ, in hope of becoming able to take a situation as organist in a village church, when her father's sudden death put an end to her plan, and altered everything.

Having lost a considerable portion of his property, he had unfortunately taken to gambling and drinking in order to drown his anxieties, and had died insolvent. The house had to be vacated, and almost all the furniture and stock in trade were sold to pay the creditors.

Friends were very kind. They raised a sum of money to help Mrs. Willington to start afresh. She was thus enabled to rent a small house, and to lay in a store of fancy articles for sale. In this way she made a home for her son, who was apprenticed in Wilminster as a lawyer's clerk. Had he not been an idle boy at school he might have done still better for himself. His elder sister, Amy, went out as a daily governess, for which she was fully qualified.

Lucy, who came between her and her brother, might have done so too, but at that time she knew of no one wanting a governess, and she felt compelled to seek some employment without delay. She would have been glad to leave the neighbourhood altogether.

In the midst of all the trouble and perplexity, good Mrs. Nixon called to see how she could help the family, and the situation before mentioned was proposed to Lucy, who declined taking it, hoping for one of a higher order. At last, meeting with nothing to suit her, she reluctantly wrote and offered herself to Mrs. Nixon, should the place still be vacant. Lucy received a very kind reply in the affirmative, and accordingly she went to Ivy Lodge, having much to learn.

"I can but give it a trial," she thought to herself; "and in the meantime something better may turn up. I shall be on the look-out."

It need scarcely be said that such conduct was dishonourable, being unfair to her mistress, whom Lucy should have acquainted with her intention from the first, that Mrs. Nixon might have an equal opportunity of looking out for *herself*.

Lady Dalby had a house ten miles off. Lucy having heard that she was inquiring for a lady's-maid, gave notice to her kind mistress, as has been already stated.

Not having been accustomed to work, Lucy Willington had found it very trying to be a servant. It was not by any means that she had too much to do; the fact was, she hated to be in a subordinate position, and where the other servants regarded her as but little superior to themselves. Mrs. Nixon had tried to enlist their sympathies for Lucy, and had expressed the wish before she came that they would do whatever they could to make her comfortable in her altered circumstances. They had felt sorry for the young woman, and had endeavoured to show her all the kindness and respect in their power; but every attention was so coldly received, being taken as her due, that the girls became disheartened, and too much inclined to "pay her back in her own coin," which was more than Lucy could stand. Therefore she gave notice to leave as soon as she heard of the situation at Lady Dalby's and obtained the place, going to it from Mrs. Nixon's.

Lucy found it necessary to make herself agreeable to her new fellow-servants, although with most of them she held her head very high.

It was not long before Lady Dalby came to live in Wilminster, when Lucy was invited to join the Bible-class. Her mistress asked her if she would like to attend it. Lucy paused, then drew herself up, and said—

"No, my lady, thank you; I'd rather not, unless it is your ladyship's wish that I should go."

"You do as you choose, Willington, on a Sunday afternoon; but I think it would be a nice thing for you. I should advise your going."

"I've never been to anything of the sort, your ladyship."

"That is no matter. Perhaps it is time you should go. Mrs. Lester is very good and kind; you may be glad to know her."

"Please, your ladyship, are all the young women such as you would like me to mix with?"

"Oh, I know nothing about that. Mrs. Lester would not invite you to a class where they were not respectable. You need not be more than civil to them, I suppose. They may be in a lower station to the one in which you were brought up, and I dare say many of them have less knowledge, but what of that? You must not be too particular."

The next Sunday, to please her mistress, Lucy went to the Bible-class. She was rather handsome, and very striking-looking, with a manner which would have appeared graceful and dignified to the rest of the class if it had not told them very plainly that they were not good enough for her. She left immediately after the closing prayer, in order to have as little to do with them as possible."

On her return Lady Dalby inquired how she had enjoyed the afternoon.

"If it please your ladyship," was the reply, "I do not wish to attend that Bible-class again. I have never been accustomed to associate with people in that rank of life."

"Very well, Willington; but you have to mix with my other servants, as you did with Mrs. Nixon's."

"Your ladyship will pardon my saying that that is entirely different. Your servants are superior to many in the Bible-class."

"I rather wish, Willington, you had not gone at all. It is such a reflection on Mrs. Lester's class to attend it once and not afterwards."

Lucy, however, was persuaded to go again, for Mrs. Lester met her during the week, and spoke so kindly to her, knowing what trouble Lucy had had, that the girl was won over, and went to the class the next Sunday. She seemed more attentive to what Mrs. Lester said, but, in other respects, was the same as before.

She continued her attendance there, and by degrees she grew more sociable with some of the young women. Elsie's lameness, and the attention shown her by the rest, attracted Lucy's notice. She became interested in her; and, finding that Elsie was in the position of a dressmaker, and not a servant, sought her friendship, and was thus drawn into acquaintance with two or three others. In time, she had the good sense to see that it was foolish to keep entirely aloof from the greater number of the girls, and that it would be pleasanter to make herself one of the party; but though Lucy learnt to stand less upon her fancied dignity, she never would consort, in those days, with the younger members of the class, nor with such as were apparently second-rate servants.

After all, she had nothing to be proud of, seeing that the lowering of her circumstances had been brought about by the misconduct of her poor father; but it is very difficult for some people to come down in life gracefully. Her mother had been only a servant. When she married, her husband and she had things in a very small way. As business prospered, they did not care to remember how limited their means had been, but brought up their children with high notions, to do very much as they liked, and please themselves.

The failure and death of her husband were a terrible blow to Mrs. Willington and her family. It was not surprising that Lucy felt service to be drudgery and humiliation, taking into account her bringing up, nor was it any wonder that, though already acting as maid to Lady Dalby, she yet made inquiries about two or three situations where a governess was wanted. None of these suiting her, she remained where she was, often building castles in the air and planning great things for herself; outwardly pleasant to her amiable mistress, but really feeling discontented and unhappy.

Lucy was particularly fond of attending St. Hilda's church, a very fine building in Wilminster, where the service was similar to that of a cathedral. She loved to look at the grand and massive pillars, which still stood in their appointed place, notwithstanding the lapse of centuries, and whilst successive generations of worshippers had passed away. She liked to see the sunlight shining through stained-glass figures of patriarchs, prophets, and apostles, and casting gorgeous colours on stately arches or ancient monuments. She gazed with a pleasure, ever new, at the fine oak carving of the stalls and the vaulted roof; but when the thrilling strains of the noble organ, blended with voices of white-robed choristers and singers, in sweet response, or canticle, or psalm, Lucy felt almost carried out of herself to some heavenly region of loveliness and glory. What a treat it was to hear the anthem! the music so wonderfully adapted to the pathos or glowing rapture of the sacred words! What feeling those beautiful intonations called forth! and the "Amens" were like the harmonies of nature on a bright summer's day, when bird, and bee, and murmuring rill combine to utter their Creator's praise.

Lucy had been to the service at St. Hilda's one Sunday, and was coming away with the crowd, in a state of mental exaltation.

"I could stay here all day," she thought, "such angelic music! That of heaven must be delightful! What a blessed thing religion is, after all! How contemptible, and how much to be pitied, those people are who don't care to attend fascinating services like these!"

A girl passed before her whom she knew. "Well really!" Lucy said to herself, "if I couldn't dress better than that, I'd stop at home! All the colours of the rainbow about her too!—Why, Mrs. Mercer has surpassed herself! What an erection of a bonnet, to be sure! Oh, how that woman is pushing me! Do take care!" which last words were spoken aloud with angry tone, whilst Lucy's cheeks flushed

crimson, and she glanced furiously round. People
would not go fast enough.   How tiresome they were!
and how annoyed she felt!   She could have knocked
that little urchin down who turned round to look at
her, and then trod on her toes!

Poor Lucy did not seem to be carrying away much
that was profitable from the worship in which she
had been engaged.   She did not appear to have been
made more humble, loving, or patient by it, notwithstanding all her high-flown feelings.   Had she indeed
been worshipping God, or was it merely that she had
been captivated by the music, and that her taste for
the beautiful in art had been gratified?   " They that
worship God must worship Him in spirit and in
truth," whether in a magnificent building or in a
shed, whether with music or without it.

Time passed on, and there came the dawning of a
new light into Lucy's mind.   She began to see that
the temple of her soul had been desecrated and defiled
by sin, and that self had reigned there all along instead of Christ.   At last she saw that that temple
could only be cleansed by " the blood which cleanseth
from all sin," and a day came when that blood was
applied, self dethroned, and Christ exalted to His
rightful position in her soul.

How different was her worship afterwards!   It was
spiritual, because inspired by the Spirit of God.   It
led to holiness, because it was the lifting up of her

heart in prayer and praise to the holy Father, through the holy Saviour, by the power of the Holy Ghost. Formerly it had been nothing more than the indulgence of natural taste for all that which charmed the eye and ear in the house of God, and which left her in reality no better than before. Her admiration of fine architecture and music still remained, but the mere gratification of it no longer satisfied her as once it had done, or at least, as Lucy thought it had.

The change in her views and feelings came about in this way. After attending Mrs. Lester's class a few Sundays, Lucy arrived at the conclusion that something which *she* did not possess was enjoyed by her teacher. Restless and discontented as the poor girl then was, a longing took possession of her, which increased to a craving, for that which would satisfy the desires of her soul, the "aching void" which nothing seemed to fill. Whenever opportunity offered, she went, first to this prayer-meeting, then to that church service, or to something else of a religious kind, but did not find the peace she sought.

Weeks and months passed by, and Lucy was still groping in the dark, when a mission was held in Wilminster. The preaching she heard impressed her greatly. She felt herself a lost sinner, and saw, for the first time, her utter helplessness. She had always clung to the idea that there was a preparatory work to be done by her, in order to make herself acceptable to Christ. Now Lucy saw how much she had been mistaken. She longed for the love of the Lord Jesus. The beauty of His character attracted her as it had never done before. Would He, could He, accept such an one as she?

No matter who saw her, Lucy determined to stay behind, and talk it all over with the mission-preacher, and thus take advantage of the general invitation to those who were anxious. He was enabled to remove some of her difficulties, and she returned to Lady Dalby's much encouraged. After two or three conversations with him, the simple truth of the gospel was understood by Lucy and enjoyed. She wondered she had never seen its meaning before. How clearly Mrs. Lester had put it, and yet Lucy had not taken it in! She now saw that her mind had been blinded by the false idea that her salvation would have to be a joint work between the Saviour and herself. Yet, after all, Mrs. Lester's Bible lessons and quiet talks with Lucy had not been in vain, in that they had led her to desire that spiritual blessing which was reached out to her by the hands of another. She now perceived that Jesus Christ Himself was the Supply for all the wants of her soul; that, by His death, He had made atonement for sin, and that in heaven He was pleading the merits of His finished work on behalf of His people; she had but to receive Him into her heart, and nothing less would do; and Lucy felt she could do no less than gladly admit the loving Saviour. Henceforth she could say—

> "My heart is resting, O my God,
>   I will give thanks and sing:
> My heart is at the secret source
>   Of every precious thing."

> "I came to Jesus, and I drank
>   Of that life-giving stream,
> My thirst was quench'd, my soul revived,
>   And now I live in Him."

She found herself introduced into a state of freedom. What a different thing life became to her after this! Earnestly did she desire to live for the time to come, not unto herself, but unto Him who died for her and rose again.

K

CHAPTER XII.

" Men call you fair, and you do credit it,
 For that yourself you daily such do see ;
 But the true fair, that is the gentle wit
 And virtuous mind, is much more praised of me,
For all the rest, however fair it be,
 Shall turn to naught, and lose that glorious hue ;
 But only that is permanent and free
 From frail corruption, that doth flesh ensue,
That is true beauty, that doth argue you
 To be divine, and born of heavenly seed ;
 Derived from that fair Spirit from whom all true
And perfect beauty did at first proceed.
 He only fair, and what he fair hath made ;
 All other fair, like flowers untimely fade."
        —SPENSER.

MOST of those who read these pages will have seen beautiful brooches, rings, and other expensive trinkets set with precious stones, such as the emerald, garnet, and turquoise, displayed in the windows of jeweller's shops. A few of my readers may have admired necklets of pearls, or coronets of rubies, or of diamonds sparkling with brilliant rays of light.

Such costly gems can only adorn the rich ; but there is an ornament which is far more valuable, and

which may be worn by the poorest servant girl no
less than by the Queen upon her throne.

All do not possess it; and with some it shines
more brightly than with others. While the wearers
may be unconscious of being decked with this lovely
jewel, they themselves can best appreciate its softened
light in the faces of their companions.

There were those in Mrs. Lester's Bible-class who
wore this charm; as a rule, they were the most
plainly-dressed young women there.

Necklaces, bracelets, and glittering gems may be
highly prized and much admired by human eyes, but
this decoration is of great price in the estimation of
God Himself, for it is " *the ornament of a meek and
quiet spirit.*"

It cannot be bought with money like earthly
jewels, for its beauty is of a higher order, consisting
in humility, gentleness, modesty; modesty as seen in
the look, manner, language, dress—in fact, in the
whole conduct.

Sad, indeed, is the defect where these sweet graces
are wanting, for nothing can take their place. All
true followers of Christ possess them in a greater
or less degree, but, independent of Christian grace,
some characters are naturally more humble, gentle,
modest than others, reflecting the beautiful ornament,
which, in the highest sense, they cannot call their
own.

Whatever Alice Sharman's attractions were, and she had her attractions, she yet was long without the crowning graces of which I have spoken, and her reflection of them was faint, and grew less and less discernible. It was only through sorrow and suffering that she became possessed of the ornament, which is the gift of God, and, unlike earthly beauty, incorruptible.*

Alice was the daughter of a respectable bricklayer's labourer at Wilminster, where she was in service. She was a member of Mrs. Lester's Bible-class, and nineteen years of age, at the time of which I am about to speak. She was good-looking, with rather a fine figure. Poor girl! If others thought her pretty, she considered herself *very* pretty; if friends told her she had a good figure, she admired it as *graceful*.

Alice seldom gave anything to her poor, hard-working parents, for whom she ought to have felt a daughter could not do enough; all her earnings were spent on dress. Her mind, in leisure moments, was chiefly occupied in devising what sort of bonnet, hat, or other attire she should buy, to set herself off to the best advantage. No one could be long in Alice's company without seeing where her thoughts were; this was made evident by the conscious looks, and the frequent putting to rights of her ribbons, collar, or necktie.

* 1 Peter iii. 4.

She did not seem to pay much heed to Mrs. Lester's lessons and warnings. After the Bible-class, she would giggle, and talk in a foolish, trifling way with anybody who would walk with her. At first, some of the girls were attracted by her pretty appearance, and inclined to be giddy too; yet even these, for the most part, soon grew tired of her tittle-tattle, which was almost entirely about her own dress or that of other people, or else she would tell of the young men who paid her attention.

Mrs. Lester asked Alice to her house for a little conversation, fixing a time; but, though apparently agreeing to the plan, the girl never meant to go, and made some excuse for not having done so when next she came to the class.

After several vain attempts to see Alice alone, Mrs. Lester stopped her one Sunday, when the girls were leaving the house. Alice coloured, and said she could not stay that afternoon.

"We are rather earlier than usual in closing," said Mrs. Lester, "but if your time is more limited to-day, I will only keep you five minutes."

Feeling obliged to remain behind, Alice agreed to what her teacher said, as the quickest way out of the difficulty; but the girl cared not for the loving Saviour of whom Mrs. Lester spoke, her heart being too full of vanity and the things of this world to have room for thoughts of Him.

On leaving the Bible-class, she had some distance to walk, and most of the girls dispersed in different directions, after going together for a little while.

Granchester, once a Roman camp, was a garrison town adjoining Wilminster. Soldiers often wandered in its streets. On the Granchester Road were pretty gardens, which were thrown open to the public on Sundays. Here also, lounging on the seats, or strolling about, soldiers were not unfrequently to be seen. The idle girls of Granchester and Wilminster, who always admired their scarlet coats, were very fond of this resort on a Sunday afternoon, and much enjoyed what they considered harmless flirtation with the young privates, who seemed equally to appreciate the company of the lasses; but although many of these silly girls meant no more than a little pleasant intercourse or amusement, it often led to real evil. They generally knew nothing of the characters of the lads and men who addressed them. Agreeable manners and lively chat sometimes prepared the way for further acquaintance, and this not seldom resulted in a foolish and unhappy marriage at the best; too often, alas! in sin and disgrace.

Alice had become very free with some soldiers, laughing and talking loudly with them, when they joined her and walked off with her. She was also heard making joking remarks to other young men, who joked with her in return. All sense of modesty and propriety was being quickly cast away.

Her plan with regard to any well-conducted girls she knew was, at first, to endeavour to hide her conduct from them, but when this could no longer be done, she became insolent and haughty. Alice had never been regular in her attendance at the Bible-class, and had now quite left off coming. There were those in it who felt it only right to speak of her behaviour to Mrs. Lester, who called to see her, and related what was said of her, which she angrily denied; but Mrs. Lester stood her ground, spoke very solemnly to the foolish girl, and warned her of the danger she was incurring.

Whilst thus engaged, Alice's mistress came in, saying, "Excuse my interrupting you, Mrs. Lester. I hope you find my servant punctual in going to your class?"

"I am sorry to say she has given up coming for some time past, Mrs. Neale. She has never been regularly."

"How is this, Alice?" said her mistress, turning to her. "You know I wish you to attend Mrs. Lester's class, and there is nothing whatever to prevent you."

"I fear she is not so steady as she ought to be," said her teacher. "I have been told by several, whom I can trust, of Alice's walking with soldiers, and of her familiarity of manner towards them. I came here to-day purposely to speak to her on the subject. It is right you should know about it, especially as she has denied the charge. I am truly sorry."

The girl looked ready to drop through the floor.

"I knew nothing of this, indeed! and am very glad you have informed me, Mrs. Lester. I am grieved to hear it. It is hard when we do all we can to make our servant comfortable, and give her religious advantages, that she should abuse our confidence and disappoint us in this way."

"Yes; it is very trying. I hope Alice will think over what I have been saying, that she will confess to her unsteadiness, and ask the Lord to help her to act differently for the future."

"I cannot keep her unless she acknowledge her misconduct, and except she turn over a new leaf. I must have some talk with her myself. Her parents shall hear about her."

This roused Alice, who begged with tears that her father and mother might not know. Although very reluctant before, she was now ready to promise anything, so that the matter should be kept quiet from them. Her mistress gave her a month, during which time Alice would be under restrictions, and closely watched; then, should she again be found conducting herself in the same unsteady manner, her parents would be informed, and she would be sent home. Her behaviour was so far satisfactory, whilst the month of trial lasted, that Mrs. Neale could discover nothing to find fault about; she therefore allowed Alice to stay. Gradually, however, she returned to her old practices.

Friends had kindly warned her mother and father with regard to their daughter. They had rather indignantly refused to believe all that was told them, but one after another again hinted that they had better keep a sharp look-out after her, and then, at last, something of her conduct was witnessed by themselves.

First one parent, and then the other, called to see the thoughtless girl, to talk to her about her giddy and disgraceful ways, and beg that she would give them up; but she endeavoured to turn aside their warnings and entreaties; at first by affected merriment, saying that young people couldn't do without their larks and bits of fun; she reckoned her father and mother took to the same when they were her age; and they couldn't "put an old head on young shoulders."

"Alice," her mother said, "your father and I may have been foolish in our time, the more's the pity! and the more anxious we are that you should be different; but, I'm thankful to say, I never went on as you do with the lads. You know we don't want you to be dull, but we do wish that your fun should be sensible-like. If you will go on in this fashion, you'll get into worse mischief; that's sure."

The girl then sought to make excuses, saying that some young men had pressed her to join them, and wouldn't let her have any peace till she did, and that when she had tried to get off, one or another would come to fetch her.

"Why did you let them know your times of going out? It's a poor sort of a reason this, your trying to get off going with these fellows. Why didn't you tell your mistress? She would have sent them to the right-abouts; but there! I s'pose that would have let her too much into your secrets, and she might have given you notice. I must have some talk with her about it."

"Oh don't, mother! Please don't;" but Mrs. Sharman wisely told all she had heard and seen to Mrs. Neale, begging her to overlook the past, and to give Alice a further trial. The lady was, at first, decided to part with the girl, and her mother had to plead very hard that her daughter might still be allowed to remain in her situation. At last Mrs. Neale consented, on the consideration that it would be very bad for Alice to be out of employment in Wilminster.

The young woman was called in, and spoken to on the subject most seriously. She seemed to

soften down, in a measure, and promised to be more
steady in future.

"You made this promise before," said Mrs.
Neale, "and yet how you have disappointed me!
It must not be so again, or I shall dismiss you
immediately."

For a time after this no fault was found with
Alice; but, little by little, she threw off all re-
straint, and became so unsteady and so insolent to
her mistress, that one day Mrs. Neale sent her
home, feeling that she could not bear the girl to be
in the house for another month, for she only grew
worse instead of better. The parents were of course
much distressed, but not surprised.

Alice Sharman might have been ruined, both for
this world and the next, but for a circumstance
which suddenly put a stop to her giddy course.

An annual fair was held in a village near Wilminster. Contrary to the wishes of her parents,
Alice walked off to it, promising to return home
before dark. She was decked out in her smartest
attire, and was soon joined by some of her frivolous
companions. At the fair was a dancing booth.
She needed no persuasion to enter it, and whilst
there time passed more rapidly than she supposed.

As Alice did not come back, her father went to
fetch her, but she managed to keep out of his
sight, and one of her friends told him that she had

left the place an hour ago, so he retraced his steps, anxiously wondering what could have become of her. The rain had begun to fall heavily, and the night was very dark.

Time wore on. Alice enjoyed it all at first, but afterwards was only too glad to escape from the wild merriment of the company. Thoughtless and giddy though she was, yet even she had been shocked by the language which had reached her ears. Bad words and profane expressions had been spoken in her hearing before, but never till now had she heard so much evil-speaking, nor seen so much drinking and vulgarity. The unhappy girl became frightened and disgusted, and at last, unable to stand it any longer, she tore herself away from her half-intoxicated companions, leaving them to think that she was only going to speak to a friend, and would then return.

Heated with dancing, Alice hastened out of the village, alarmed at the lateness of the hour, dreading what her parents would say, and feeling somewhat conscience-stricken for her conduct to them. She was lightly clothed, and the night, besides being wet, was cold and windy. Being too tired to keep up a rapid pace for any great distance, she grew more and more chilled, and on reaching home the poor girl was shivering with cold and fatigue.

The anxiety of the parents was very great. Alice's father had been in search of her in various quarters. Her mother had long had the supper ready, but neither she nor her husband could eat anything. Poor Mrs. Sharman sat by the fire, white and trembling; at every sound going to look out at the door into the street. The rain was blown by gusts of wind against the window panes. "What a night for the child to be exposed to!" sighed her mother. "There's nothing more to be done, as far as I can see," said her father, and they waited in dreary suspense.

At length the latch was lifted, and Alice appeared, drenched with rain, and looking jaded and miserable.

"Here you are at last!" said her mother. "How terribly anxious you have made us!" and she burst into tears.

Alice sobbed helplessly, as her mother began to remove some of her girl's wet things.

"What on earth have you been about?" said her father. "Here have I been backwards and forwards after you for the last three hours. How could you use us so?"

Alice only cried the more.

"Come! stop this, and tell me where you've been. Do you hear?"

"I've only been to the fair and the dance."

"Then where were you when I came there, and they said you'd left an hour before ? "

" I was there."

" It's no good your telling me what isn't true, for I mean to know all about it."

" Let it wait till to-morrow," pleaded the mother. " She must take off her damp clothes. Her boots are soaked."

The father was by no means inclined to wait for an explanation, but he was at length persuaded to let the matter rest until the morning.

The next day, however, found his daughter too ill to leave her bed.

A long and severe illness followed, and although she recovered from it, it left a weakness of the heart, to which she was ever afterwards subject.

The worst symptoms being alleviated, Alice had leisure to think. She noticed her mother's worn and anxious face, as she patiently and carefully nursed her day after day. The sick girl knew that it was a great struggle to her mother to " make both ends meet," with the additional burden of this illness, for what little remained of Alice's wages was soon gone. Her father, too, looked ill and troubled. She became truly sorry for the distress and anxiety she had caused her parents by her giddiness and self-will. Alice began to see how heedless she had been of their wishes, and how little she had ever thought of helping those to whom she owed so much.

As soon as the invalid was sufficiently restored to health to give an account of the night of the fair, without danger of suffering from the narration of things which were depressing to remember, she told her parents all about it, and they were satisfied that the statement was true. She expressed her sincere sorrow for her conduct.

Mrs. Lester and other Christian friends visited Alice. She at length became deeply convinced of sin, and earnestly desirous of living a life worth living; for she realised now that her former years had been sadly wasted, and that little was left of them but painful memories. What a mercy her illness had not ended in death!

She saw what a snare vanity had been to her, and how her great aim in the past was to appear attractive and to be admired, more especially by the soldiers and lads she met. Alice had worshipped self, and courting flattery, had been deceived by it. She now felt truly thankful to have been preserved from utter ruin, considering how the warnings of her parents, friends, mistress, and teacher had been slighted by her.

Recollections of the Bible-class brought softening thoughts with them. Alice remembered how Mrs. Lester had often dwelt upon the words, " that *who-*

soever believeth in Him should not perish, but have eternal life." Could "whosoever" include *her*—a poor, sinful girl like herself? Here was a ray of hope.

How she wished she had been more regular in attending that Sunday-class, and had valued the teaching more! What a golden opportunity it now appeared, and an opportunity which might never come again!

"How different I might have been," she said to herself, "if I had been guided by what was taught me there! but I paid very little attention to those Bible lessons!"

This verse, however, learnt in childhood's days, seemed to force itself upon Alice's memory, holding out the hope that even she might be forgiven of God, because it said, "*Whosoever* believeth in Jesus should not perish," and she knew that all will perish in hell unless forgiven. Then, too, the text went on to say, that those who believe "shall have eternal life." This was stronger still; meaning that they shall not only escape hell, but that they shall be brought to heaven.

Alice had no idea where her own Bible was, so she looked for the verse in her mother's large baize-covered one, till having found the words, she read the whole of the 3rd chapter of St. John. To her delight the missing Bible was afterwards discovered.

It had been put away on a high shelf, for she had never cared for it before. Now, in her anxiety, Alice longed to become acquainted with it. She began St. John's Gospel, read on, and thought it over day after day. The result was, that she learnt to rest on the promises of God, and to know that she had eternal life, being "born again, not of corruptible seed, but of incorruptible, by the Word of God, which liveth and abideth for ever." The distress of mind vanished like a mist before the rising sun, and joy and peace came through believing. The words of the hymn were realised by her—

> " Now none but Christ can satisfy,
> None other Name for me !
> There's love, and life, and lasting joy,
> Lord Jesus, found in Thee ! "

It was soon manifest to others that Alice was indeed "a new creature" in Christ, for it was seen that "old things" had "passed away," and that "all things" had "become new."

Her parents, who had been troubled by her depression, were glad to find how much happier she was, though they themselves had been unable to guide her to the peace she sought.

Alice's illness left her very delicate, and repeated attacks resulted in her becoming a confirmed invalid, but not an unhappy one. Sickness of body is sometimes the means of healing to the soul. The cup

L

of earthly sorrow has often been made to convey the purest joy. So it had proved with her. Grieved as her parents were at her long-continued affliction, she was now a greater comfort to them than ever before, entering into their sorrows and perplexities, as far as possible endeavouring to help and cheer them by her brightness, and her loving words and ways.

She did not hide the Source of her happiness, and she earnestly prayed that her father and mother might enjoy the same rest and gladness.

Alice took in needlework, and when able would make little things for Mrs. Lester's missionary basket.

Ill - health greatly altered Alice's appearance. The bloom of complexion soon faded away, and her face grew thin and lost its youthful look, whilst her eyes told the tale of an enfeebled constitution; but in the place of what is usually considered pretty and attractive, there was something far more worthy of admiration. It was beauty of character, which showed itself in a modest, gentle, thoughtful expression which lighted up Alice's face, and gave a charm to it, such as no brilliant complexion, no plaits of golden hair, nor even beautiful eyes, without the graces of mind and heart, can ever give.

The ornament, of which mention was made at the

commencement of this chapter, had been cast aside by Alice Sharman as mean and worthless, but now it appeared adorning her with a softened brightness, a heavenly light, such as had never graced her in her gay and careless days.

CHAPTER XIII.

"Stand up, stand up, for Jesus,
   The strife will not be long;
This day the noise of battle,
   The next the victor's song:
To him that overcometh,
   A crown of life shall be;
He with the King of glory
   Shall reign eternally."
                              —G. DUFFIELD.

ANNIE BENNETT had made confession of her faith in Christ to Mrs. Lester, and to the members of her Bible-class; but the dying girl felt that this was not enough. She wished to speak to her aunt and uncle, her own relatives. And this she shrank from most of all, yet was she anxious to do so, and that soon; so Annie prayed and watched for a fitting opportunity, when she could see one or the other alone.

The next day, after she had finished her letter, her uncle was at liberty to spend part of the evening with her, whilst Mrs. Sheldon took occasion to do some ironing, and to employ herself in various household matters.

Annie began by saying in a very nervous way, "I shall not be here much longer, Uncle James."

"O lassie! I don't like to hear ye say that," and he drew the back of his brawny hand across his eyes.

"Well, I'm going to a better home, Uncle—a right good one!"

He paused, then said in rather a hurt tone of voice, "Your aunt and I have all along tried to give ye a good home, my girl."

"Oh yes, Uncle, you have indeed! and I love you dearly." It was an effort to her reserved nature to express so much affection, which, with the gratitude welling up in her heart, and the fear of paining him, made her cheeks burn and her eyes fill with tears. "Both you and Aunt Emma have always been so kind to me. I wish I could thank you for all your goodness, but "—— her voice trembled, "I feel it all, I'm sure, though I can't talk about it." She put her handkerchief to her eyes, and tried to stifle a sob.

"Come, little Nan, I can't stand this!" the poor man spoke with a choking voice, while he rose and looked out of the window.

Annie soon regained her composure. The sweet text, which had cheered and strengthened her before, was helping her again by its words of encouragement,—"Fear thou not; for I am with thee: be not dismayed; for I am thy God: I will strengthen thee; yea, I will help thee; yea, I will uphold thee with the right hand of my righteousness."

"Uncle James," she began, "I'm loth to say 'Good-bye' to you. Parting's hard work; but I want you to promise me something; will you?"

"Yes, Annie; if so be I can, I will, without a doubt."

"Then it's this—I want you to say that you'll meet me in heaven."

"I hope, dear, we shall all find each other up there—to be sure I do; but what's the good of my *promising* to meet you in heaven?"

"It just comes to this, Uncle. I ask you to seek Christ for yourself. For some long time I desired to have Him for my *Friend*, but I didn't wish to have Him for my *Saviour*, not thinking that I needed Him to save me; and yet I felt I couldn't have Him for my Friend without taking Him as my Saviour first, so I wasn't happy; but one Sunday I heard a sermon on the text, 'A Friend of publicans and sinners.' God made it plain to me through that sermon that I was a lost sinner, and in need of a Saviour as much as the worst. I sought Him for myself, and ever since I have had Him for my Saviour and my Friend."

Annie paused. A long coughing fit was the consequence of her having said so much. It had been a great effort to her to say what she did, and that had been in broken sentences, for the difficulty of breathing had increased. Her uncle did not speak for some time, except to express his sympathy with her as regarded the cough.

At last he said, " I don't know why you should class yourself, nor me either for the matter of that, with the worst sinners. God Almighty is merciful, and I can't ever think that He'd send folks to hell who've always been respectable, paying their way and doing harm to nobody. Reason enough why thieves and drunkards, and such like, should reap the wild oats they've sown ; but there's some considerable difference betwixt us and them."

" Excuse me, Uncle Jim ; not in the way of being saved, for God says, ' there's no difference ' there, ' for all have sinned, and come short of the glory of God,' and ' the soul that sinneth it shall die ; ' but He also says that when we believe in the Lord Jesus we have everlasting life. I can show you places in the Bible where He tells us those things, if you've a mind I should."

" My dear child," said her uncle, " I believe in Jesus Christ, and have done so all my life. I was brought up to it."

" I used to think so too," said Annie, after a pause ; " but now I believe very different to what I did then. I didn't *trust* Jesus then ; but now, I've found that each one of us has to seek the Saviour for himself or herself, just as if there was nobody else to be saved. Would you mind reading me a chapter, uncle?"

"No, dear; more if you like. Only it strikes me you've talked till you're tired out, and so the best thing you can do is to settle yourself to have a nap."

"Well, the 3rd chapter of St. John, please; and then I'll lie still."

When it was read, Annie pleaded, "Uncle, you'll think of that chapter when I'm gone; won't you?"

He kissed her, and pressed her hand. Presently he said, "Here comes your aunt. What will she say to your looking so tired?"

She did think the poor girl looked sadly worn out, and was ready to blame Uncle Jim for letting her become so fatigued.

The next day Annie endeavoured to make use of the opportunity she had of speaking to her aunt, but Mrs. Sheldon tried to ward off any conversation of a religious kind, having heard something of what had been said the night before.

"Auntie," the invalid remarked, in a faint voice, "I'm afraid you get very weary with nursing me, what with your other work as well; but I shan't keep you much longer at it."

"My poor Annie!" her aunt said, "I shall miss you sadly. I'm real glad to do what I can for you," and she wiped her eyes with the corner of her apron. "Don't you be bothering yourself about me," she continued, "but lie still, and let me read you to sleep. You mustn't excite yourself again, as you did last night when uncle was with you."

"Will you read me the 3rd chapter of St. John, Aunt Emma?"

"Yes, my dear; what you like, so long as you keep quiet."

The chapter having been read aloud, Annie said, "Auntie, do think of that 16th verse; it's for you."

"Very well, dear. Now I shall leave you for a time."

Annie sighed heavily. She knew not how to speak to her aunt about the better things, but made several attempts to do so afterwards, when Mrs. Sheldon turned the conversation, or avoided it in some way, just as the poor girl was making a beginning. All that could be done under these circumstances was to put her difficulty into the Lord's hands, and then, in faith and patience, to watch for the opportunity which He was sure to give.

Annie had now no expectation of recovery. In fact, she was longing to go home, and waiting in cheerful submission for God's time to come.

In the spring, indeed, she had cherished hope of returning health. The warm sunny days in April had revived her, and rallying so much as to be able to sit out of doors, Annie thought she was recovering. The doctor said that the month of May would try his patient, but that, if she could pull through it, she might linger on awhile.

The bright summer had come and passed away, when she had often been well enough to sit in the porch, which was covered with honeysuckle and climbing roses, or under the yew-tree hedge, with her work, or Bible, or some book that had been lent her. However, before the autumn had appeared, Annie had gradually been growing weaker and weaker, and now it seemed that the time could not be long. Shocks of golden grain had been gathered in from the corn-fields which sloped down to the cliff, and which could be seen from the casement window of her room; but Annie's spirit was still waiting to be carried home to the heavenly garner. Her cough, which had been troublesome all along, had become worse, and her breathing also.

Some days had elapsed since she last attempted to speak to her aunt, when one morning Mrs. Sheldon, being more at liberty than usual, was sitting with Annie, who began by saying, "Dear Aunt Emma, I shan't be able to talk to you much oftener; let me say a few words. You won't hear many more from me."

"Well, dear," said her aunt, unable to resist

such an appeal, and feeling a choking in her throat, "don't tire yourself."

"Auntie, I do wish to meet you in heaven," the sick girl said, taking Mrs. Sheldon's hand, "I want you to seek the Lord Jesus for yourself. I came to Him as a lost sinner, and He has saved me. You must come in the same way. He says, 'Him that cometh unto me I will in nowise cast out.'"

"What do you mean by *coming to Jesus*, Annie?"

"It's believing on Him; it's trusting Him; it's letting Him take us and make us His; or there's another way of putting it, it's just receiving Him into our hearts; and such a grand Visitor as He is! No, He's more than a visitor—He comes to *dwell* in our hearts, when we invite Him there; for you know, Auntie, we are His of right, because He has bought us with His blood."

"But then, we are told to come to Jesus by prayer."

"Yes, Aunt Emma, but we must come in faith, because the Saviour died in our place, and now lives to plead for us with His Father; so, as it were, taking *His* name, we may go to God in prayer, and He will welcome us and bless us. If we don't go believing, trusting in Jesus, we don't rightly go to Him at all."

"Well, dear, I always say my prayers, at least

once a day, unless there's anything particular to prevent: and then, you know, I've always accustomed myself to go to church."

"Yes, but are you ready to die?"

"Well, my dear, I can't quite say that; but I'm not going to die yet, I hope."

"O Auntie! who can tell? It isn't safe to put off seeking Christ." After a pause, and colouring much, Annie said, "Don't be offended, Aunt Emma, but did you ever see yourself a sinner in the sight of God?"

Courage had indeed been gained since Annie first attempted to say a word for Christ.

Mrs. Sheldon did not look pleased. She said hurriedly, "Oh, of course! we know we're all sinners."

Her niece saw she had said about as much as her aunt could bear, and only remarked further, that when she felt sin a burden, she came to the Lord Jesus to have the load removed, because He is the Lamb of God, who died to take away the sin of the world.

After a short silence, Annie said, "I wish I knew how to thank you, Aunt Emma, for all your goodness to me since mother died; but I'm bad at that sort of thing. I do feel it, though I can't speak out as I would."

"My dear child!" said Mrs. Sheldon, kissing her,

"don't you say a word more about it. You know how glad we've been to have you, and you've always been a good girl to us. We shall miss," she began, but tears prevented her finishing the sentence.

Annie tried to say what might be comforting, but she too broke down.

Presently she said, "I should like those in the Bible-class who have been so kind to me to have, each of them, a little remembrance. Would you bring me those books, and my desk and workbox, Auntie?"

"No, my dear, not now. You must rest. In the afternoon, when you've had a sleep, you shall have your things."

"Very well, Aunt Emma. Nobody could be more careful over me." The poor girl sighed wearily, and a terrible coughing fit was the consequence of so much talking.

After a time, her aunt brought Annie her little valuables, and left the room. With a trembling hand, the invalid wrote in the Bible which had become so precious to her, Mrs. Sheldon's name, and a text, putting marks against several chapters. Uncle James' name was written by Annie in her prayer-book and also in her hymn-book; and she marked some of her favourite hymns for him, and wrote down a text in one of the books. During the latter part of Annie's illness, in compliance with her wish, it had been arranged that Mr. Armitage should visit her. He came, not only at stated times, but as often as his other engagements would allow. These visits were greatly enjoyed by Annie, who grew less and less reserved each time he called, and he was much pleased with her state of mind.

Though very weak, she lingered on, to the surprise of all, growing thinner and more feeble still.

One day she said to Mr. Armitage, " Please, sir, I've a request to make. You've been truly kind and good in coming to see me; but there's yet one thing I wish for so much before I go.'

"What is it, Annie?" he asked, seeing her nervous look.

" Well, sir, I've been thinking how I should like to take the Lord's Supper."

" I shall be very happy to administer it to you," he said. Mr. Armitage had been hoping that she would express a desire to receive the Holy Communion, believing that it would prove a great comfort and help to her. He inquired if she had ever partaken of it.

"Never but once, sir; that was just after I was confirmed."

They had some conversation about it, and then Mr. Armitage arranged to come the following Monday, that they might commemorate the Saviour's dying love—a love which is infinite, eternal, unchanging. Mrs. Lester would be able, the next Sunday, to invite friends in the Bible-class to join them in keeping the blessed memorial feast.

Their teacher liked to encourage as many of her class as valued the privilege, and were prepared by a true and enlightened faith to unite with her occasionally in partaking of the Lord's Supper. At such times, they met at her house before going to church, and after singing a hymn together, she made a few remarks on some suitable passage of Scripture, and led her young friends in prayer.

Annie's room being small, also to avoid the excitement of her seeing too many at once, those who were permitted the opportunity of uniting with her in the service of Holy Communion were divided into two parties; so that should she still remain a little longer, and wish to partake of this sacrament again, they who had not joined with her on the first occasion, might be ready to do so then.

On the day appointed, Mrs. Lester met Elsie Dale and two others of her class, at Wilminster station, and the train conveyed them, in a few minutes, to Waterend. They took the path across the fields, and were not long in reaching Mrs. Sheldon's house, when they were shown upstairs.

Annie was raised in bed with pillows, and looked very calm and happy; although the hectic flush on her thin cheeks, and the more than ordinary brilliance of her dark eyes, bespoke excited feeling. She appeared pleased to see her friends, as they quietly greeted her.

The time spent in that sick-room need scarcely be described. It will be enough to say, that the devotion there expressed was reverent and heartfelt, and that His sacred presence was enjoyed, which makes any house the house of God; and this, not by the dying girl alone, but by those who had come to share the feast of joy with her. Whilst waiting for Mr. Armitage's coming, a sweet hymn was sung, and Mrs. Lester's short and earnest prayer was the language of every heart. She concluded with the petition that all might meet at " the Marriage Supper of the Lamb."

Annie was comforted and strengthened by the Saviour whose wondrous act of love she was then specially calling to mind, and thus feeding her soul on the thought of His death, which was represented by the broken bread and the wine poured out ;— *His death*, which trusted in for salvation, becomes the entrance to everlasting life, by freeing us from eternal death, and bringing us into union with the Risen Saviour, who is our Life.

Mrs. Lester went the next day to inquire after Annie, and found that her cough had been very bad, and that she had had a restless night. Hear-

ing that she was awake, Mrs. Lester went upstairs
to spend a few minutes with her.

"It was a very happy time yesterday," Annie
said; "I was glad, ma'am, that you were with us, as
well as some of those who have been so kind to me
in the class. It was so nice, too, that Mr. Armitage
was the clergyman."

"There are others in the class, dear Annie, who
would like to join with you, should you be spared to
partake of the Holy Communion again."

"I should enjoy it, Mrs. Lester, if God's will I
should stay here a little longer, and if Mr. Armitage
will be good enough to come again to give it me."

Annie did yet linger on for a while, rallying after
this; and Lucy Willington and three other friends
were not disappointed. Before long, however, it
became evident that their former companion was
nearing home. Her breathing was very bad. Her
cough had almost gone. She could speak but little,
and that in tones which were scarcely audible.

Mrs. Sheldon had become more thoughtful in
manner, and though she did not say much, sufficient
was said to raise the hope that she was taking her
niece's words to heart, as well as those of Mrs. Lester
and Mr. Armitage, for both the latter had spoken to
her at Annie's request.

Uncle James, too, had said something which encouraged the dying girl to think that he was be-

ginning to see himself a lost sinner, in need of the
only Saviour from sin.

As for her, she was patiently waiting, and resting
on the promises of God in Christ; in joyful, longing expectation of being with Him whom her soul
loved.

. . . .

> "   . . . They saw the smile
> He passed away in, and they said, ' He looks
> As he had woke and seen the face of Christ,
> And with that rapturous smile held out his arms
> To come to Him.' "   —JEAN INGELOW.

The sun rose in brilliance one September morning,
but Annie's sun of life had set to this world.

> " The message came for her, and fearlessly
> She answered to its summons, ' Here am I !'
> Safe, safe for ever, now ; no weary days,
> Or sleepless nights of pain—no night is there."

She had entered the " abode of those who die in the
Lord Jesus, that abode where joys which cannot be
expressed are the heritage of a youth which knows
no decay."

On the following Sunday Mrs. Lester spoke about
her to those in the class.   Many were the tears shed
by the young women who knew, and had learnt to
love, the gentle girl.

She had evidenced to them that, trusting in her
loving Saviour, she was supported by His realised

presence through weakness, suffering, and death, and was thus enabled to glorify Him in the night of earthly sorrow, showing forth His praise, not only with her lips but in her life; that is, *in what remained to her of life,* for it was then like a declining shadow.

Christians owe it to their Lord and Master, to speak for the honour of His Name, and thus confess to their faith in Him; but no confession of Christ will avail, unless backed up by a consistent life.

As many of the Bible-class as could be spared wished to follow Annie's remains to their last resting-place, the next Tuesday afternoon, having contrived to put on mourning for the occasion. They met at the railway station, took the train, and then walked to Mrs. Sheldon's house. Mrs. Lester, also, came to pay this last tribute of affection to Annie. Not a few had brought flowers to drop into the grave, and several beautiful wreaths were placed on the coffin. The sight of the motionless burden seemed to make her friends realise that their former companion at the Bible-class was indeed gone from them for ever, as regarded this world; but they knew it was well with her; and there were some present who had a confident expectation of meeting her where " adieus and farewells are a sound unknown." Before leaving the grave all joined in singing a sweet and appropriate hymn.

Annie Bennett teaches us that those into whose hearts the light of life shines, may not hide it. Christians must be light-bearers, for the glory of God and the benefit of those around them. The Saviour says to them, "Let your light so shine before men, that they may see your good works, and glorify your Father which is in heaven." A lighted lantern might be covered with a metal case, but if so, who would be the better for it? No one could either admire the light, or be guided by it. Christians are intended to be like lanterns *un-covered*, as lamps of clear glass, letting the bright rays shine through them into the surrounding darkness, to lead to Jesus and to heaven.

Annie had hidden her light for a time, and, not confessing Christ, was not fully happy; but when her conscience was roused by the Holy Spirit to see the ingratitude of this course, she was strengthened, by "looking unto Jesus," to make a bold confession of her faith, on various occasions, to her relatives and friends.

This witness for Christ was not borne without much painful effort to deny self. She found it necessary to dwell in thought, again and again, on the Almighty power with her and *in* her, till she grasped the truth, "I can do all things, through Christ who strengtheneth me."

Neither was Annie's testimony given without

much earnest supplication for the guidance and help of the Holy Spirit; her faith grew by exercise; and in gracious answer to her believing prayer, her faithful God and Saviour carried her through every opposing influence.

Afterwards, in looking away from herself, in trying to forget her feelings of shyness, nervous fear, and reserve, and to remember Him who had helped her, she was enabled to rejoice more than she had ever done before, for "in keeping of" His commandments "there is great reward."

Could Annie's voice be heard, would she not say to each young Christian friend, " Be not thou ashamed of the testimony of our Lord?" (2 Timothy i. 8).

CHAPTER XIV.

"In a service which Thy love appoints
  There are no bonds for me,
For my inmost heart is taught the truth
  That makes Thy children free;
And a life of self-renouncing love
  Is a life of liberty."   —MRS. WARING.

AFTER life had become to Lucy Willington a very different thing to what it had been, and was no longer disappointing and insipid, but inspired by new energies and glorious hopes, she felt quite contented to remain in service, believing that God had placed her there, that in it He might be glorified. She determined not to seek a higher position until He opened out the way.

"What has come to you, Willington?" said Lady Dalby; "you look ten times happier than you did a week or two ago!"

Lucy related in short what had passed; and, though her mistress said but little in reply, she thought much about it.

Some servants, whilst not meaning to be unkind to their mistresses and the families they serve, do not take into consideration how to avoid what will be inconvenient to their employers, nor in what way they can give them comfort and pleasure. Lucy, however, had never been inconsiderate for her mistresses, with the exception of having left Mrs. Nixon as has been described.

One day Lucy saw her, and expressed her sorrow for her behaviour then, and told Mrs. Nixon the circumstances which had led to such a happy change in her views and feelings generally. Mrs. Nixon was truly pleased to hear the good tidings Lucy had to tell.

Henceforth her service was a service of love, and therefore she could not fail to find pleasure in it, whilst taking an interest in her duties, working with a will, and more than ever considering the wants and wishes of her mistress. Was it any wonder that the latter became increasingly attached to Lucy? Lady Dalby could not but see that religion had done much for her maid. Love to God, and desire to please her Heavenly Master, lay at the root of it all.

Lucy grew pleasanter to her fellow-servants, becoming kinder and more sympathising, and no longer holding herself aloof as she had done. Her manner towards all was much softened and more humble, even to the younger and poorer members of the Bible-class.

After two or three years, at the request of the
clergyman whose church she attended, Lucy took a
class at the Sunday-school. Sorry as she was to
give up going to the Bible-class, she yet was pleased
to have some special work to do for Christ, remembering the injunction, " Freely ye have received,
freely give."

Lucy's sister had done well as a governess, im-
proving herself in various ways. She acquired a
better style of teaching, and consequently was able
to take a superior situation. One day she came to
see Lucy, and press her to give notice to leave Lady
Dalby, feeling sure of obtaining for her sister the
higher position of governess, before very long. Lucy,
however, declined to part from her kind mistress,
to whom she was really attached, for no other than
a selfish reason, as it then seemed to her; yet who
could have blamed her had she taken her sister's
advice, and so sought a sphere where such powers
and acquirements as she already possessed could be
brought into use ?

A year after this, Mrs. Clarke, with her three
little ones and their nurse, came to stay with Lady
Dalby. The children caught the whooping-cough,
in addition to which, the baby became very ill with
congestion of the lungs. As he needed the greatest
care, his mother and nurse alternately sat up with
him at night. Lucy willingly offered to take her

turn also, which help was thankfully accepted. The child was recovering, but required constant attention, when his sister was taken dangerously ill. Lady Dalby did her utmost to spare Lucy, who took entire charge of the baby at night, and frequently also during the day. She was invaluable. They did not know what they should have done without her during that time of anxious watching.

The children recovered. Their mother wished, in parting, to make Lucy a present as some little return for her kindness, but she would receive nothing.

"We owe baby's life in great measure to you, Willington; it will give me much pleasure if you will accept this money by way of acknowledgment."

Lucy assured the lady, in thanking her for her kind thought, that she had been very pleased to give whatever help lay in her power, and had felt it a privilege to do so.

"Then is there anything I can purchase for you?" asked Mrs. Clarke.

"There is one thing I should like, ma'am. If I am not making too bold, may I ask for a photograph of the dear children?"

"Certainly," said the lady; "I am so glad you have mentioned it. I shall have their likenesses taken before long, and will send you one of each."

In about two months' time came some beautiful

coloured photographs, nicely framed, with a grateful note, and a handsomely bound book, which Lucy could not but accept with pleasure. She had learnt unselfish kindness from the best Master, even from Him who gave Himself for us.

We all have our trials sooner or later. Sometimes the faults of days long gone by visit us with bitter consequences. Happy as Lucy had become, pleasant as her situation was with her gentle mistress, she had family troubles, and now and then her course lay through rough waters.

An old woman in Wilminster had borne a grudge against Lucy's father, having never forgiven him for not taking her part with regard to some charity. Mrs. Bond secretly rejoiced over the fall the family had sustained, and made cutting insinuations and allusions to the pride of former years. Lucy knew of this, and felt it trying; but had the unpleasantness spread no further she would not have concerned herself much about it. Mrs. Bond, however, had a granddaughter, who was acquainted with a girl attending Mrs. Lester's class. In consequence, poor Lucy became the subject of unkind tittle-tattling, and of exaggerated and false reports. There was a strong impression against her by some of those who had been her companions in the class, and whom she frequently met with, though no longer a member of it. Those who knew her best neither could nor would believe any harm of Lucy, but did all in their power to uphold her and to overcome the ill-feeling and prejudice of others. It is, notwithstanding all efforts, very difficult to destroy a false report, although only too easy to set one afloat.

> " Who steals my purse steals trash ; . . .
>
> . . . .
>
> But he that filches from me my good name
> Robs me of that which not enriches him,
> And makes me poor indeed."

Dear friends, let us take care lest we thoughtlessly and unintentionally detract from the character of another ! and let us beware of *listening* to reports which may be utterly untrue ! The man who shall " dwell ‘on high," in a holier atmosphere than the rest, lifted above the undue depression of anxiety and trouble; who shall be defended from evil, and whose wants shall be supplied, is that man of God who, whilst living and speaking consistently with his profession, also " *stoppeth his ears from hearing of blood,*" and " *shutteth his eyes from seeing evil* " (Isaiah xxxiii. 15, 16).

Lucy often met Mrs. Parker, the young woman who had made so much mischief. She would pass her by with a haughty look, or begin whispering, perhaps, to some companion evidently about her. Lucy had once ventured to speak to Anne Parker with regard to her trifling and giddy conduct in church, which reproof, though kindly meant, had been ill received, and made Anne the more bitter in her opposition. Lucy, however, had the patience and courage to live it all down, and the false-witnessing and unkindness of the girls in the class recoiled upon themselves.

One morning Lady Dalby said, "Willington, I want you to go to Sunnyside to inquire of the housekeeper how Mrs. Leslie found her poor sister. Go as soon as you have dined, as I shall delay my letter till I hear."

Lucy had nearly reached the house, which was a little way out of the town, when her attention was arrested by the screams of a baby and the barking of a dog in a cottage standing alone. Hearing no one speak, and thinking the child was being frightened by the dog, she entered the outer door, which was not shut, and giving a rap, opened the inner one, when, to her dismay, she saw that a small linen-horse, full of clothes, had been knocked down. The top was resting on the cradle, in which the baby lay, whilst the other end had fallen into the fender, and was on fire. Another minute, and the cradle would have been blazing too. Lucy hastily drew it away, and with a real, though unspoken, cry of "Lord, help me!" she endeavoured to rescue some of the clothes by throwing the burning articles into the fender, and those not yet on fire to a distance. This was difficult, as they had become entangled with the horse in falling.

Regardless of the pain of her scorched fingers, she did her best to prevent more harm from following. The horse had begun to set the floor on fire; but help was near. The mother, who had gone to a neighbour's for a pail of water, was returning; hearing the barking of the dog and her child's screams, she hurried home. Rushing in, she saw the alarming state of things, and immediately poured the water on the burning linen, horse, and floor, and thus stopped further mischief.

Now that Lucy's work was done, her strength failed. She just managed to throw herself into a chair, and then fainted away.

The young mother caught hold of her and supported her, which was all that she could do, till Lucy had revived a little, when the woman reached her a glass of water.

The poor girl looked up, meeting the sorrowful gaze of Anne Parker, and appeared at first rather startled.

" Did ye know who you were lending a helping hand to ?" asked Mrs. Parker.

" No," said Lucy faintly ; " I'm glad if I've been of any use to you."

" *Use*, indeed ! You've been the saving of my baby. I mind me where the cradle was. D'ye feel better now ? "

" I shall soon, thank you."

Anne Parker hastened to make Lucy a cup of tea, which she tried to drink, but was still feeling very faint and trembling, when an empty fly passed the door. The young woman stopped the driver, and Lucy was glad to return in the carriage, a neighbour who had joined them insisting on going with her.

" You'll look in upon me soon ?" asked Anne Parker, shaking hands with Lucy. " I shall want to know how you get on. You've been terrible kind."

" I shall be glad to come as soon as I can get an opportunity," was the reply.

In the meantime Lady Dalby was wondering why Lucy did not appear, and was a little annoyed that she had to send off the letter before Mrs. Leslie's account of her sister arrived.

" I have never known Willington treat me in this way before," the mistress said to herself. " She usually comes back when she is expected. What can it mean ? "

Lady Dalby was still more surprised when she saw her maid step out of a fly, and enter the house, taking hold of another woman's arm, and looking ill. The lady anxiously inquired what was the matter. It was soon explained, and Lady Dalby was as kind and thoughtful for Lucy as might be supposed.

Two days after she went again to make the inquiry for her mistress, and to look in at Mrs. Parker's.

" Don't hurry," said Lady Dalby. " If the woman should ask you, you can stop and have a cup of tea with her."

Anne Parker was pleased to see Lucy. Her kindness had made the young woman feel ashamed of the ill-natured and inconsiderate things she had said of her ; and having some good feelings in her disposition, Anne now wished to do whatever lay in her power to make amends for the past.

" I hope you soon got all right again ? " she asked. " Poor baby wouldn't have stood much chance but for you."

" I felt pretty well the next morning, thank you ; and am quite brisk to-day."

" You got your hands burnt, didn't you ? "

" Yes, a little. I'm obliged to keep this one tied up in cotton-wool for a few days ; but it's not nearly so painful as it was, now that the air is excluded."

" That must be awkward for you, as you're a lady's-maid."

" Yes ; only my mistress is so good, and will not let me use it much. I tell her ladyship I'm not so helpless as she thinks."

Lucy made light of her discomfort, but some of

her fingers were sadly scorched and blistered, as well as the inside of her hand.

"I've been wanting to see you," Anne Parker said. "I know I haven't been kind. I've laughed at you, and said what I'd no call to say about you. I never could have thought you'd have humbled yourself to be so good-natured when the horse was a-fire. I hope you'll forgive all, and try to forget the past."

"Say no more about it, Mrs. Parker," said Lucy.

"I shall never speak against you again," continued the young woman. "Granny shall hear all, and I hope she'll change her tune—leastways she ought. You know she took against your family, mostly because poor Mr. Willington didn't support her about the almshouses."

"Yes; but never mind. It's no manner of use remembering these things which have gone by. We will let them be bygones. I fear you lost a great deal of linen last Wednesday?"

"True enough, I did. I was vexed, and no mistake, when I came to look at it; and the more so as it was all my own fault. I knew the horse didn't stand steady, and so I ought to have left it more safe, and then the dog wouldn't have knocked it down."

"Will you take this half-crown to help you to buy some new clothes?" asked Lucy.

"No, Miss Willington, thank you. That's too much indeed! It's over good of you," said Anne Parker, with a look of surprise, and colouring as she returned the money.

"Oh, do take it; I shall be so pleased," entreated Lucy.

"Well, to be sure! and after the way I treated you! and after all your kindness the day before yesterday, and your getting your fingers burnt, and the fainting! No, I couldn't do such a thing; but thank you all the same."

"If you really had rather not accept the half-crown, then I will not press you," said Lucy, intending to lay it out in a small purchase for Mrs. Parker.

"You won't be offended, Miss Willington? My husband gets good wages. Do come and see me sometimes."

Lucy promised to do so, and then made the conversation turn upon the subjects she was longing to speak about, saying how much happier she had been since she had come to the Lord Jesus, and had laid her sins on Him.

"I was very proud," Lucy added, "till God taught me something of myself; and I still have to watch and pray with regard to this special temptation to pride, as well as to many others. I don't wish to set myself up as better than you, Mrs.

N

Parker; I only want you to remember that what
God is doing in one heart, He is able and willing to
do in another. He is ready to work in us what of
ourselves is impossible."

"You're most wonderfully good, I'm sure," was
the reply; "but I shall never come up to you."

"No, no, Mrs. Parker; don't say so, please," said
Lucy, in a beseeching tone.

"Oh, but you're so humble! Any one can
see "——

"I wish to be humble," interrupted Lucy, "but
you know, Mrs. Parker, to be humble is only to
have a *true* idea of ourselves; and we can never
learn *how* bad and weak we are. It is those who
realise that they have much forgiven, who love
much."

"Well, anyways, I know I'm bad."

"Yet God cares for you. It was He who sent
me just in time to save the baby from being
burnt."

There was a pause. Anne Parker thought about
what had been said. Lucy had obtained a great
influence over her, and gained a promise from her,
that, if her husband would stay at home with the
baby, she would meet Lucy the next Sunday evening, and go with her to church. For some months
before this, Anne had given up attending any place
of worship. She and Lucy walked together to God's

house that Sunday night, for the first, but, by no means, the last time.

As Lucy had opportunity, she went to see Mrs. Parker, who improved greatly, becoming more gentle and quieter, both in manner and dress.

One day, about six months after the fire, Lucy had gone in to have a cup of tea with her, when Anne began by saying, " I've something to tell you, Miss Willington. My husband's taken a house ten miles from here, and we shall have to be off next Thursday. I'm that grieved to think of going away from you! You've been such a friend to me," said the young woman, with choking voice and starting tears.

" Oh, dear! I am sorry you have to go," replied Lucy; " but we must hope to meet again now and then."

"I shall write and tell you how we get on, as soon as I can."

" Yes, do; I shall be so glad to hear from you."

A fortnight later came a letter from Mrs. Parker, which was expressed in this way :—

"MY DEAR MISS WILLINGTON,—You will be pleased to hear we've got things straight in our new house, and like it very well. Robert has heaps of work to do, and he takes to the place. Baby is all right, except for cutting his teeth, and sends kisses to you. I don't like to think of not seeing you here. It makes me feel fit to fret, and crying's no good; but, dear Miss Willington, I know *now* where to find comfort. It was your Christian conduct that day when the clothes-horse caught fire that taught me ever so much. Afterwards, too, you kept on teaching me the same lesson, when you was just as kind, although I'd behaved so bad to you in the past, and you knew everything about it. Also it's what you've said now and again, and your taking me to church, that have led me to seek the Saviour you serve, who invites us all to come to Him. I'd a great mind to tell you of this, but I didn't know how; so, thinks I, I'll write and mention it, and thank her kindly: but there!—the worst is, I'm bad at saying how much I feel beholden to you. I often try to thank the good Lord for it all, and for sending of you to learn me. Robert, in general, reads his Bible with me at night now, and we have a prayer together, out of a little book that's been given us. We've taken to keeping a few fowls, and I hope to send you a little present of eggs, as soon as they begin to lay.—With love, I remain, yours gratefully,

Anne Parker."

Thus Lucy Willington overcame evil with good. How different she had become to what she once was! True religion had softened and ennobled her character. She had grown in grace, training herself by loving service, in habits of unselfish care for others; and in this way winning far more love and respect, from all whose opinion was worth having among her acquaintances, than in times of greater prosperity.

After a while, Lucy was married to a young man worthy of her, who had known her from childhood, and who, like herself, had learnt to "walk by faith," and "not by sight." He quickly made his way in business, and Lucy's circumstances became better than they had ever been before.

As her new home was a considerable distance from the Sunday-school, she felt compelled to give up teaching there; but it was not long before she commenced a Bible-class, of which several of the members were her former scholars.

This work was a source of great interest to Lucy, and a means of blessing, both to the teacher and to those she taught, for the promise never fails, "he that watereth shall be watered also himself" (Prov. xi. 25).

CHAPTER XV.

"With good will doing service, as to the Lord, and not to men."
—Eph. vi. 7.

"Behold, as the eyes of servants look unto the hand of their masters, and as the eyes of a maiden unto the hand of her mistress; so our eyes wait upon the LORD our God."—Ps. cxxiii. 2.

"O our God, ... we have no might against this great company that cometh against us; neither know we what to do: but our eyes are upon Thee."—2 Chron. xx. 12.

"Looking unto Jesus."—Heb. xii. 2.

> "Look away to Jesus, 'mid the toil and heat,
> Soon will come the resting at the Master's feet;
> For the guests are bidden, and the feast is spread:
> Look away to Jesus, in His footsteps tread."
> —Rev. H. BURTON.

ONE autumn evening at Wilminster there was a large gathering in a brilliantly-lighted room which opened into the museum of curiosities. Long tables were spread for tea, down the centre of which beautiful hot-house plants were ranged. The many bright faces present were chiefly, but not altogether, those of young people; for some were there whose youth was fast passing away, and a few among them had already attained to middle-age. The occasion of it was, that the various Bible-class teachers of Wilminster had agreed to unite in giving a tea to their classes.

The members of each class sat together, and the hissing urns were presided over by the teachers and their helpers. There were three or four classes of lads and men, but all the rest were those of girls and women.

After tea, music and the singing of an efficient choir contributed greatly to the pleasure of the evening. This part of the entertainment took place in an adjoining room. At the same time, the spacious museum was lighted up, and thrown open to the guests. Kind friends and teachers accompanied them there, and endeavoured to interest them in the curious relics of days gone by, as well as to explain the meaning and use of curiosities from India, China, Japan, Africa, the South Sea Islands, and other parts. Most of the visitors had not even been inside the museum before, and those who had previously seen it, had never much understood or appreciated the objects there displayed till now; so that when the bell rang to summon all into the music-room, there were many young people who felt somewhat reluctant to leave the museum.

After the company had joined in singing a hymn, a clergyman, who acted as president, said a few words by way of introducing an important feature

of the meeting. The teachers had been requested
to choose their own subjects, and prepare short addresses, to be read aloud by the president towards
the close of the evening. A fair proportion had
responded to the appeal, and their papers were heard
with great interest and attention. "Friendship,"
"Temperance," "Prayer," "Bible Study," were
amongst the chosen themes. Hymns were sung at
intervals between the addresses. With two of the
latter we will draw to a conclusion. Those selected
are, the one written by Mrs. Steel, formerly Lucy
Willington, on "Service;" and that by Mrs. Lester
on "Unconscious Influence."

Lucy was sitting near a door at the lower end of
the room, and was glad to escape during the reading
of her composition, but returned shortly afterwards.

" SERVICE.

" Dear Friends,—I feel, in some measure, qualified
to write on the subject which I have taken, because,
as some here present may remember, it is only a
few years since I was a servant myself. Owing to
circumstances, I was compelled to accept this position, from which I greatly shrank, it being quite
contrary to my naturally proud feelings and ideas.
Still, I am thankful to say, I have lived to know
that this was the best training for me.

"I had not been many months in service before

my views regarding it altogether changed; and I hope I may humbly and gratefully say, that I was led to see all things in a very different light to what I had ever done hitherto. I now saw that when God places us in service, though it may be a more lowly station than that which we have left, yet, in so doing, He does not degrade us, for there is nothing really degrading but sin. I began to find that I could be very happy as a servant. I speak to many who are in service, and I would say, *Do not be ashamed of being servants.*

"In these days, when many are seeking great things for themselves, let us consider Him, who, when on earth, was amongst His disciples as 'He that serveth;' and that He 'made Himself of no reputation, and took upon Him the form of a servant,' and, though Lord of glory, He 'came not to be ministered unto, but to minister.' Can service be otherwise than honourable, when *He* submitted to it, and condescended to take the lowest place?

"You will recollect that, before He entered upon His public ministry, He worked in the carpenter's shop at Nazareth. His sacred hands must have held, His fingers used the hammer, the chisel, and the plane.

"The night of His betrayal, our Heavenly Master set us an example of loving humility. He was then about to endure the utmost shame for us, by dying on the cross, and thus to descend beneath our sin to

the lowest depths of suffering, 'to raise us to His
throne.'

"He had gone to eat the Passover in the upper
room prepared for Him and His disciples, amongst
whom had arisen a strife as to which of them should
be the greatest in His kingdom of glory, which they
were expecting to be established immediately. It
would seem that no menial was present, as was
customary, to wash the feet of the assembled guests,
although water, basin, and towel had been provided. None of the twelve were willing to do the
part of servant to the rest; and, therefore, their
Lord and ours arose, and took it upon Himself.

"He did not, and could not forget His high position; were this possible, we are still reminded that,
at the very moment when He laid aside His garments, girded Himself with a towel, poured water
into a basin, and washed the feet of His disciples,
*He knew that He was come from God, and went to
God! Yet He was not ashamed to take the place of
the humblest menial of the household.* Shall we be
content that our Master should have set us such an
example, whilst we refuse to perform acts of lowly
service, or are discontented with our calling? Let
us remember His words, 'Whosoever will be great
among you, let him be your minister (or *servant*);
and whosoever will be chief among you, let him be
your servant' (or *slave*).

"I do not dwell upon the fact of the Lord Jesus becoming the Servant of the Father to redeem fallen humanity, for in this we cannot follow Christ, except to draw from the subject the lesson St. John enforces, that, in remembrance of His love in laying down His life for us, 'we ought to lay down our lives for the brethren.'

"Dear friends, whether engaged in domestic service or not, *every one of us* is in effect a servant, for God has made us all dependent upon one another.

"*How* are we to serve? *Faithfully.* We must be faithful to the trust committed to us, whatever it may be.

"*How* are we to serve? *Wisely*, in the best way possible, under all circumstances.

"*How* are we to serve? *Lovingly;* and this will make all service willing service, therefore pleasant to ourselves, and acceptable to those we serve. In itself, it may be *un*pleasant, but, rendered out of love, it will be done cheerfully, if not with pleasure. *There is freedom in loving service.* It delivers from the tyranny of self, and, adding to beauty of character, is thus part of God's training of His children for His glory. *He* gives the power to serve faithfully, wisely, lovingly. 'With good-will doing service, as to the Lord, and not to men.'

"*Our Master and great High Priest, though in heaven, is still serving the interests of His people.* As their Mediator, He is thinking of them, watching over them, feeling for them, supplying their need, defending them from evil, keeping them unto life eternal. A day is approaching when He shall 'gird Himself, and make them to sit down to meat, and will come forth and serve them.' He says, 'If any man serve me, let him follow me; and where I am, there shall also my servant be.'

"The homeliest, most commonplace service, done from love to the Master, will not be unrewarded then; for He adds, 'If any man serve me, him will my Father honour.'

"Oh that, to each one of us, the words may be spoken, 'Well done, good and faithful servant, enter thou into the joy of thy Lord!'"

The addresses were, for the most part, without signatures; but, in several instances, it was not difficult for the members of the various classes to discover which papers were written by their respective teachers; some being humorous, others grave; some short and pithy, and others more discursive. On the whole, all were much appreciated.

"UNCONSCIOUS INFLUENCE.

"We all know how greatly we are influenced by people around us, as well as by the circumstances through which we pass. We speak and act toward each other, with the express purpose of producing certain effects on the minds and conduct of those with whom we have to do.

"Perhaps, however, we are none of us sufficiently aware of the extent of influence we are exerting *unconsciously.* Without the slightest effort on our part, those in our company are more or less swayed by this power for evil or for good which we possess. An angry, discontented, or deceitful expression of countenance acts for evil on those who see it, even when no word is spoken; whilst a loving, happy, truthful look has an influence for good. Not only so; beyond the impression which our appearance and manners have on others, the *known character* of every person tells upon those around. Dear friends, if we are indeed the Lord's people, how earnestly should we pray that our influence may be constantly on the side of good; that is on the side of Christ, of holiness, and of heaven! How watchful should we all be lest we should hinder any on the narrow road, or even keep them from entering it!

"I would ask the *young women of our Bible-classes* to remember this; for you have a power which will tell upon those with whom you associate at your classes. An earnest-minded girl, who is seeking to profit by what is taught, will unconsciously be influencing her companions to be attentive also; whilst one who is giddy and thoughtless may be injuring others, by causing them to lose the benefit of an opportunity which will never come again. Fresh opportunities may be given, but lost ones can never be recalled, nor the blessing which they would have brought, if rightly used!

"Many of you are *servants*. Bear in mind, dear sisters, the influence you will exercise for good or evil, for time and for eternity, over your fellow-servants.

"*Daughters at home*, do not forget your influence there.

"It was once said of a dwelling-place visited by the Son of God, on whom a grateful woman, full of love to Him, had poured her costly and fragrant perfume, 'the house was filled with the odour of the ointment.' So let your homes be fragrant with the sweetness of your daily lives; let it be poured forth in honour of the same Heavenly Master, and you will draw others towards Him.

"How can this holy influence be maintained— we are so weak, so sinful? By 'LOOKING UNTO JESUS.' There are some flowers which always turn to the sun. They require his direct rays to fall upon them, and would not be so healthy if kept in the shade. We are like them; we must be continually turning to the 'Sun of Righteousness;' we must keep our eyes fixed on the Lord, or we shall be but sickly plants in His garden, *if, indeed, we are there at all!* A drooping flower soon withers away; and, if our eyes are turned down upon ourselves and our earthly concerns, it is a sign of withering graces. We must look off from ourselves and our circumstances, and be ever 'looking unto Jesus,' and drawing fresh life and power from our Risen Lord.

"Some of you may have heard the fabulous accounts of the deadly upas-tree. It was said that neither animal nor plant could live, unless at a distance of many miles from it, on account of the poisonous effect it had on the surrounding air; it was, in imagination, at least, an evil influence working upon all around. There are, on the contrary, flowers which scent the air by their health-exhaling fragrance. We cannot touch a leaf of some plants, without its making known that we have been in contact with them. The Jewish rulers 'took knowledge' of Peter and John, 'that they had been with Jesus,' and He is 'the Rose of Sharon, and the Lily of the valleys.'

"The violet is an unobtrusive little flower, often hidden in its nest of leaves; but we all know the charm of its delicate perfume. Many of your lives, dear young friends, may be quiet, hidden lives, making no show in the world; but, if you are the Lord's servants, you may be diffusing a sweet and powerful influence for good, which, unlike the fragrance of the fading flower, will last, and continue to last, even when you may be transplanted from His garden on earth to the paradise above, into which 'there shall in no wise enter anything that defileth,' and where 'the glory of God doth lighten it, and the Lamb is the light thereof.'"

HELEN LESTER.

Having read the addresses, the president said a few kind and encouraging words to the teachers, and the members of their classes; and reading the 133d Psalm, he spoke, 1st, of Christian union, the work of the Spirit of God; 2d, of the holy anointing oil, to which it is compared—the element of consecration, which was unlike anything else, fragrant, and all pervading; 3d, of the fertilising dew, to which this union is likened; a dew of unfailing blessing—even eternal life.

After a prayer, in which the president besought that all present might realise this blessed union with each other, in Christ the Risen Head, our great High Priest, the doxology was sung, and all returned to their various homes and places of service, with happy recollections of a very pleasant evening.

Here we, too, must say Farewell.

PRINTED BY BALLANTYNE, HANSON, AND CO.
EDINBURGH AND LONDON.

By Mrs. MARSHALL.

The *Standard* says:—"Mrs. Marshall is one of the most popular writers
for the young. She is a master of the art of drawing children's characters."

With numerous Illustrations, and Handsomely Bound in Cloth.
Crown 8vo.

Price Five Shillings each.
CASSANDRA'S CASKET.

SILVER CHIMES; OR, OLIVE.

STORIES OF THE CATHEDRAL CITIES OF ENGLAND.

POPPIES AND PANSIES.

REX AND REGINA; OR, THE SONG OF THE RIVER.

DEWDROPS AND DIAMONDS.

HEATHER AND HAREBELL.

Price Three Shillings and Sixpence each.
MICHAEL'S TREASURES; OR, CHOICE SILVER.

SIR VALENTINE'S VICTORY, AND OTHER STORIES.

RUBY AND PEARL; OR, THE CHILDREN OF CASTLE AYLMER. A Story for Little Girls.

Price Two Shillings each.
MY GRANDMOTHER'S PICTURES.

STELLAFONT ABBEY; OR, NOTHING NEW.

MATTHEW FROST, CARRIER; OR, LITTLE SNOWDROP'S MISSION.

MRS. MARSHALL'S WORKS—continued.

Price One Shilling and Sixpence each.

THE BIRTH OF A CENTURY; OR, EIGHTY YEARS AGO.

MARJORY; OR, THE GIFT OF PEACE.

GRACE BUXTON; OR, THE LIGHT OF HOME.

THREE LITTLE BROTHERS.

THREE LITTLE SISTERS.

Price One Shilling each.

HEATHERCLIFFE; OR, IT'S NO CONCERN OF MINE.

DAISY BRIGHT.

THE LITTLE PEAT-CUTTERS; OR, THE SONG OF LOVE.

PRIMROSE; OR, THE BELLS OF OLD EFFINGHAM.

TO-DAY AND YESTERDAY:
A STORY OF SUMMER AND WINTER HOLIDAYS.

BETWEEN THE CLIFFS; OR, HAL FORESTER'S ANCHOR.

FRAMILODE HALL; OR, BEFORE HONOUR IS HUMILITY.

A VIOLET IN THE SHADE.

LIGHT ON THE LILY; OR, A FLOWER'S MESSAGE.

A ROSE WITHOUT A THORN.

A CHIP OF THE OLD BLOCK:
BEING THE STORY OF LIONEL KING, OF KINGSHOLME COURT.

By R. M. BALLANTYNE.

With Illustrations. Crown 8vo. 5s. each.

The BISHOP of LIVERPOOL has said :—

" Your books for the young are standard and classic with me. I give all of them to my children as fast as they come out, and recommend them to all my friends."

THE ROVER OF THE ANDES: A Tale of Adventure in South America.

THE YOUNG TRAWLER: A Story of Life and Death and Rescue in the North Sea.

DUSTY DIAMONDS, CUT AND POLISHED: A Tale of Arab City Life.

THE BATTERY AND THE BOILER; or, Adventures in the Laying of Submarine Electric Cables.

THE KITTEN PILGRIMS; or, Great Battles and Grand Victories.

THE GIANT OF THE NORTH; or, Pokings Round the Pole.

THE LONELY ISLAND; or, The Refuge of the Mutineers.

POST HASTE: A Tale of Her Majesty's Mails.

IN THE TRACK OF THE TROOPS: A Tale of Modern War.

THE SETTLER AND THE SAVAGE: A Tale of Peace and War in South Africa.

UNDER THE WAVES; or, Diving in Deep Waters.

RIVERS OF ICE: A Tale Illustrative of Alpine Adventure and Glacier Action.

THE PIRATE CITY: An Algerine Tale.

BLACK IVORY: A Tale of Adventure among the Slavers of East Africa.

THE NORSEMEN IN THE WEST; or, America before Columbus.

THE IRON HORSE; or, Life on the Line. A Railway Tale.

THE FLOATING LIGHT OF THE GOODWIN SANDS.

ERLING THE BOLD: A Tale of the Norse Sea-Kings.

THE GOLDEN DREAM: A Tale of the Diggings.

Mr. R. M. BALLANTYNE'S BOOKS—continued.

DEEP DOWN : A Tale of the Cornish Mines.

FIGHTING THE FLAMES : A Tale of the London Fire-Brigade.

SHIFTING WINDS : A Tough Yarn.

THE LIGHTHOUSE ; or, The Story of a Great Fight between Man and the Sea.

THE LIFEBOAT : A Tale of our Coast Heroes.

GASCOYNE, THE SANDALWOOD TRADER : A Tale of the Pacific.

THE WILD MAN OF THE WEST : A Tale of the Rocky Mountains.

RED ERIC.

THE RED BRIGADE.

FREAKS ON THE FELLS : And why I did not become a Sailor.

With Illustrations. Crown 8vo. 3s. 6d. each.

THE ISLAND QUEEN ; or, Dethroned by Fire and Water. A Tale of the Southern Hemisphere.

THE MADMAN AND THE PIRATE.

TWICE BOUGHT : A Tale of the Oregon Gold Fields.

MY DOGGIE AND I.

THE RED MAN'S REVENGE.

PHILOSOPHER JACK : A Tale of the Southern Seas.

TALES OF ADVENTURE ON THE SEA.

TALES OF ADVENTURE BY FLOOD, FIELD, AND MOUNTAIN.

TALES OF ADVENTURE ; or, Wild Work in Strange Places.

TALES OF ADVENTURE ON THE COAST.

BATTLES WITH THE SEA. 16mo, 2s. 6d.

SIX MONTHS AT THE CAPE : Letters to Periwinkle from South Africa. A Record of Personal Experience and Adventure. 6s.

THE COLLECTED WORKS OF ENSIGN SOPHT, late of the Volunteers. Illustrated by Himself. 1s. 6d. Picture boards, 2s. 6d. Cloth.

MR. R. M. BALLANTYNE'S

MISCELLANY of ENTERTAINING and INSTRUCTIVE TALES.

With Illustrations. 16mo. 1s. each.

Also in a Handsome Cloth Case, Price 17s. 6d.

The "Athenæum" says:—"There is no more practical way of communicating elementary information than that which has been adopted in this series. When we see contained in 124 small pages (as in *Fast in the Ice*) such information as a man of fair education should possess about icebergs, northern lights, Esquimaux, musk-oxen, bears, walruses, &c., together with all the ordinary incidents of an Arctic voyage woven into a clear connected narrative, we must admit that a good work has been done, and that the author deserves the gratitude of those for whom the books are especially designed, and also of young people of all classes."

I.

FIGHTING THE WHALES; or, Doings and Dangers on a Fishing Cruise.

II.

AWAY IN THE WILDERNESS; or, Life among the Red Indians and Fur Traders of North America.

III.

FAST IN THE ICE; or, Adventures in the Polar Regions.

IV.

CHASING THE SUN; or, Rambles in Norway.

V.

SUNK AT SEA; or, The Adventures of Wandering Will in the Pacific.

VI.

LOST IN THE FOREST; or, Wandering Will's Adventures in South America.

MR. R. M. BALLANTYNE'S MISCELLANY—continued.

VII.

OVER THE ROCKY MOUNTAINS; or, Wandering Will in the Land of the Red Skin.

VIII.

SAVED BY THE LIFEBOAT; or, A Tale of Wreck and Rescue on the Coast.

IX.

THE CANNIBAL ISLANDS; or, Captain Cook's Adventures in the South Seas.

X.

HUNTING THE LIONS; or, The Land of the Negro.

XI.

DIGGING FOR GOLD; or, Adventures in California.

XII.

UP IN THE CLOUDS; or, Balloon Voyages.

XIII.

THE BATTLE AND THE BREEZE; or, The Fights and Fancies of a British Tar.

XIV.

THE PIONEERS : A Tale of the Western Wilderness.

XV.

THE STORY OF THE ROCK.

XVI.

WRECKED, BUT NOT RUINED.

XVII.

THE THOROGOOD FAMILY.

By the Rev. A. N. MALAN, M.A.

THE LIGHTHOUSE OF ST. PETER. Small crown 8vo.

By AGNES GIBERNE.

ST. AUSTIN'S LODGE. With Illustrations. 5s.

BERYL AND PEARL. With Illustrations. Crown 8vo. 5s.

DECIMA'S PROMISE. With Illustrations. Crown 8vo. 3s. 6d.

DAISY OF OLD MEADOW. With Illustrations. 2s.

KATHLEEN. With Illustrations. Crown 8vo. 5s.

OLD UMBRELLAS; or, Clarrie and her Mother. With Illustrations. Crown 8vo. 2s.

By GRACE STEBBING.

THAT AGGRAVATING SCHOOL GIRL. With Illustrations. Crown 8vo. 5s.

HOW THEY DID. With Illustrations. Crown 8vo. 5s.

WHAT A MAN SOWETH. With Illustrations. Crown 8vo. 3s. 6d.

By H. M. DICKINSON.

THE SEED OF THE CHURCH: A Tale of the Days of Trajan. Crown 8vo. 5s.

THE CHILD OF THE CHOSEN PEOPLE. Crown 8vo. 3s. 6d.

By Miss M'CLINTOCK.

ALICE'S PUPIL. Crown 8vo. 1s. 6d.

By DARLEY DALE.

SEVEN SONS; or, The Story of Malcolm and his Brothers. With Illustrations. Crown 8vo. 5s.

SPOILT GUY. With Illustrations. Crown 8vo. 2s.

CISSY'S TROUBLES. With Illustrations. Crown 8vo. 3s. 6d.

LITTLE BRICKS. With Illustrations. Crown 8vo. 2s. 6d.

By ELLEN L. DAVIS.

YOKED TOGETHER: A Tale of Three Sisters. With Illustrations. Crown 8vo. 5s.

A BOY'S WILL. With Illustrations. Crown 8vo. 2s.

By the Rev. J. R. MACDUFF, D.D.

PARABLES OF THE LAKE; or, The Seven Stories of Jesus by the Lake of Galilee. A Sunday Book for Young Readers. With Illustrations. Crown 8vo. 3s. 6d.

THE STORY OF A SHELL. A Romance of the Sea: with some Sea Teachings. A Book for Boys and Girls. With Coloured Frontispiece and Other Illustrations. Small 4to. 6s.

THE STORY OF BETHLEHEM. A Book for Children. With Illustrations by THOMAS. Crown 8vo. 2s. 6d.

HOSANNAS OF THE CHILDREN. With Illustrations. Crown 8vo. 5s.

THE WOODCUTTER OF LEBANON. A Story Illustrative of a Jewish Institution. 16mo. 2s.

TALES OF THE WARRIOR JUDGES. A Sunday Book for Boys. Fcap. 8vo. 2s. 6d.

THE CITIES OF REFUGE; or, The Name of Jesus. A Sunday Book for the Young. 16mo. 1s. 6d.

THE EXILES OF LUCERNA; or, The Sufferings of the Waldenses during the Persecution of 1686. Crown 8vo. 2s. 6d.

THE FOOTSTEPS OF ST. PAUL. Being a Life of the Apostle designed for Youth. With Illustrations. Crown 8vo. 5s.

BRIGHTER THAN THE SUN; or, Christ the Light of the World. A Life of Our Lord for the Young. With 16 Illustrations by A. ROWAN. Post 4to. 3s. 6d.; in paper cover, 1s.

WILLOWS BY THE WATER COURSES; or, God's Promises to the Young. A Text-Book for Children. 64mo. 6d.; paper cover, 3d.

By the Rev. GEORGE EVERARD, M.A.

YOUR SUNDAYS: Fifty-Two Short Readings. Especially intended for Schoolboys. Crown 8vo. 2s. 6d.

"YOUR INNINGS:" A Book for Schoolboys. Sixth Thousand. Crown 8vo. 1s. 6d.

EDIE'S LETTER; or, Talks with the Little Folks. Small 4to. 2s. 6d.

By JOHN GREENLEAF WHITTIER.

CHILD LIFE. A Collection of Poems for Children. With numerous Illustrations. Small 4to. 3s. 6d.

"A charming volume. We know of no other which strings together so many gems of the like water."—*Times.*

P

By Rev. J. JACKSON WRAY.

SIMON HOLMES, THE CARPENTER. Crown 8vo. 3s. 6d.

GARTON ROWLEY; or, Leaves from the Log of a Master Mariner. With Illustrations. Crown 8vo. 3s. 6d.

HONEST JOHN STALLIBRASS. With Illustrations. Crown 8vo. 3s. 6d. Gilt edges. 5s.

THE CHRONICLES OF CAPSTAN CABIN. Crown 8vo. 3s. 6d.

MATTHEW MELLOWDEW. With Frontispiece. Crown 8vo. 5s.

NESTLETON MAGNA. Crown 8vo. 3s. 6d. Gilt Edges. 5s.

PETER PENGELLY. With Illustrations. Crown 8vo. 2s.

PAUL MEGGITT'S DELUSION. With Illustrations. Crown 8vo. 3s. 6d.

A MAN EVERY INCH OF HIM. Crown 8vo. 3s. 6d.

THE MAN WITH THE KNAPSACK; or, The Miller of Burnham Lee. With Frontispiece. Crown 8vo. 1s.

WIDOW WINPENNY'S WATCHWORD. With Frontispiece. Crown 8vo. 1s.

By Miss HAVERGAL.

MORNING BELLS. Being Waking Thoughts for the Little Ones. Royal 32mo, 9d.; paper cover, 6d.

LITTLE PILLOWS. Being Good Night Thoughts for the Little Ones. 32mo, 9d.; paper cover, 6d.

MORNING STARS; or, Names of Christ for His Little Ones. 32mo. 9d.

THE FOUR HAPPY DAYS. 16mo. 1s.

BEN BRIGHTBOOTS, and Other True Stories. Crown 8vo. 1s. 6d.

BRUEY. A Little Worker for Christ. Crown 8vo. 3s. 6d.

Cheaper Edition, 1s. 6d.; paper cover, 1s.

MEMORIALS OF LITTLE NONY. A Biography of Nony Heywood, who was the First Collector for the Bruey Branch of the Irish Society. By her Mother. With Preface by Miss HAVERGAL, and a Portrait. Crown 8vo. 2s. 6d.

By the Rev. WALTER J. MATHAMS.

SUNDAY PARABLES TOLD TO CHILDREN. With Frontispiece. Crown 8vo. 2s. 6d.

By Mrs. BARCLAY.

SUNDAY OCCUPATIONS FOR CHILDREN. Crown 8vo. 1s.

By Miss LYSTER.

AN UNWILLING WITNESS. With Illustrations. Cr. 8vo. 3s. 6d.

ROBIN RUN-THE-HEDGE. Crown 8vo. 1s.

By ELLA STONE.

GRACE MURRAY. A Story. With Illustrations. Crown 8vo. 3s. 6d.

By Mrs. BARBOUR.

THE WAY HOME, AND HOW THE CHILDREN REACHED IT BY A RAILWAY ACCIDENT. With Illustrations. 18th Thousand. 16mo, 1s. 6d. limp; 2s. 6d. boards.

THE IRISH ORPHAN IN A SCOTTISH HOME. A Sequel to "The Way Home." 16mo, 1s. limp; 2s. 6d. boards.

THE CHILD OF THE KINGDOM. Twenty-second Thousand. With Illustrations. 16mo, 1s. limp; 2s. 6d. boards.

THE SOUL-GATHERER. Seventeenth Thousand. 16mo, 1s. limp; cloth gilt, 2s. 6d.

By Mrs. HORNIBROOK.

THROUGH SHADOW TO SUNSHINE. With Illustrations. Crown 8vo. 2s. 6d.

LIFE'S MUSIC; or, My Children and Me. With Illustrations. Crown 8vo. 5s.

By Mrs. BAYLY.

THE STORY OF OUR ENGLISH BIBLE, AND WHAT IT COST. Crown 8vo. 3s. 6d.

By Mrs. BATTY.

MATZCHEN AND HIS MISTRESSES. Imperial 16mo. 1s. 6d.

By the Rev. DAVID MacEWAN, D.D.

THIS YEAR. Anniversary Addresses for the Young. Second Edition. Square 16mo. 1s.

By Mrs. WINSCOM.

DEAR OLD ENGLAND. A Description of our Fatherland. Dedicated to all English Children. Crown 8vo. 3s. 6d.

"English children will find much that is well worth knowing, and well told, in this copiously illustrated volume."—*Christian World.*

SUNDAY READINGS FOR FARM BOYS. Founded on the Church Catechism. With Prefatory Notice by the Right Rev. E. H. BICKERSTETH, D.D., Bishop of Exeter. 16mo. 1s.

MRS. LESTER'S GIRLS AND THEIR SERVICE. With Frontispiece. Crown 8vo. 2s. 6d.

BY THE SAME AUTHOR.

MISS MARSTON'S GIRLS AND THEIR CONFIRMATION. With Frontispiece. Crown 8vo. 2s. 6d.

EFFIE'S YEAR: A Tale for the Little Ones of the Church. With Illustrations. Crown 8vo. 2s. 6d.

AUNT EFFIE'S GIFT TO THE NURSERY. Hymns and Verses for the Little Ones. 16mo. 1s. 6d.

THE HOLY CHILDHOOD. Conversations on the Earliest Portion of the Gospel Narrative. Crown 8vo. 3s. 6d.

THE PROPHETS OF JUDAH: A Book of [Bible Teaching for Elder Children. By M. D. H. Crown 8vo. 5s.

ROSE DUNBAR'S MISTAKE; or, Whom have I in Heaven? By M. L. D. With Preface by HORATIUS BONAR, D.D. Crown 8vo. 5s.

MORAG: A Tale of Highland Life. Crown 8vo. 3s. 6d.

By J. L. WATSON.

GREY CRAIGS: A Tale of Scottish Life. With Illustrations. Crown 8vo. 5s.

By MARY R. HIGHAM.

THE OTHER HOUSE: A Tale. With Frontispiece. Crown 8vo. 2s. 6d.

By SARSON C. J. INGHAM.

DR. BLANDFORD'S CONSCIENCE. Crown 8vo. 5s.

By ROSE PORTER.

IN THE MIST: A Tale. With Frontispiece. Crown 8vo. 2s. 6d.

By the late Lady K. SHUTTLEWORTH.

THE LADDER OF COWSLIPS; or, What is Sound? Cr. 8vo. 2s.

"An ingenious and pleasing attempt to make the rudiments of music intelligible and attractive to beginners. There is much thought and graceful meaning worked into this unpretending but very useful little book. It will help beginners over some difficult places, and bring out the beautiful meaning which lies in what to their eyes may seem only dry and difficult." —*Athenæum*.

By W. H. G. KINGSTON.

ROGER WILLOUGHBY; OR, THE TIMES OF BENBOW. With
Illustrations. Crown 8vo. 5s.

"A capital story, but especially notable for the short Preface, perhaps one
of the most earnest and touching in its simplicity that was ever prefixed to a
book of this kind."—*Guardian.*

By the Rev. J. H. WILSON.

THE GOSPEL AND ITS FRUITS. A Book for the Young. With
Illustrations. Crown 8vo. 3s. 6d.

OUR FATHER IN HEAVEN: The Lord's Prayer Familiarly Explained and Illustrated for the Young. With Illustrations.
Crown 8vo. 2s. 6d.

By Miss HELEN PLUMPTRE.

SCRIPTURE STORIES; or, Sacred History Familiarly Explained
and Applied to Children. 16mo.

Moses, 1s. 6d. Joshua, 1s. 6d.

By the Rev. RICHARD NEWTON, D.D.

THE BEAUTY OF THE KING. With Illustrations. Crown 8vo,
2s. 6d.

By ANNA LEHRER.

SOLDIERS AND SERVANTS OF CHRIST; or, Chapters of
Church History. With Preface by the Rev. F. V. MATHER,
M.A., Canon of Bristol. Crown 8vo. 5s.

By the Rev. JAMES WELLS, M.A.

"Mr. Wells possesses in large measure a gift which is by no means
common—that of engaging the attention and stirring with sympathetic
emotions the heart of the young."—*Nonconformist.*

BIBLE ECHOES: Addresses to the Young. Crown 8vo. 3s. 6d.

THE PARABLES OF JESUS. With Illustrations. Crown 8vo. 5s.

BIBLE CHILDREN. Studies for the Young. With Illustrations.
Crown 8vo. 3s. 6d.

BIBLE IMAGES. With Illustrations. Crown 8vo. 3s. 6d.

By Rev. T. S. MILLINGTON.

UNDER A CLOUD. With Illustrations. Crown 8vo. 2s. 6d.

By Mrs. ALLNATT.

MAMMA'S BIOGRAPHIES FROM THE CHURCH SERVICE
CALENDAR. Crown 8vo. 3s. 6d.

By ELEANOR C. PRICE.

HIGH AIMS ; OR, ROMANTIC STORIES OF CHRISTIAN ENDEAVOUR. Crown 8vo. 5s.

By L. T. MEADE.

A LONDON BABY : The Story of King Roy. With Illustrations. Crown 8vo. 2s. 6d.

"Very touching and sad, though the end is happy."—*Athenæum.*

THE CHILDREN'S PILGRIMAGE. With Illustrations. Cr. 8vo. 5s.

"Displays the author's well-known power of vivid conception of character, and clear, graphic description. The story is full of incident and adventure."—*Literary Churchman.*

By EVERETT GREEN.

LADY TEMPLE'S GRANDCHILDREN. With Illustrations. Crown 8vo. 2s. 6d.

By the Rev. W. A. C. CHEVALIER.

WILLIAM LONGE OF WYKEHAM; or, The Winchester Boy. A Story of the Boyhood of William of Wykeham, in Five Scenes and a Prologue. Illustrated with Etchings. Crown 8vo. 2s. 6d.

By Mrs. PRENTISS.

URBANE AND HIS FRIENDS. With Illustrations. Crown 8vo. 2s. 6d.

AVIS BENSON ; or, Mine and Thine. And other Tales. With Illustrations. Crown 8vo. 2s. 6d.

THE HOME AT GREYLOCK. Crown 8vo. 2s. 6d.

OUR RUTH : A Story of Old Times in New England. With Illustrations. Crown 8vo. 2s. 6d.

By Lady HOPE.

A MAIDEN'S WORK. Crown 8vo. 5s.

TOUCHES OF REAL LIFE. Crown 8vo. 5s.

SUNNY FOOTSTEPS ; or, When I was a Child. Fcap. 4to. 3s. 6d.

By Mrs. HOWARD.

A SUMMER IN THE LIFE OF TWO LITTLE CHILDREN. With Illustrations. Crown 8vo. 3s. 6d.

By Mrs. PROSSER.

"OAKBY" AND "NUMBER TWENTY-NINE." With Illustrations. Crown 8vo. 2s. 6d.

By B. HELDMANN.

DORRINCOURT: A Tale for Boys. With Illustrations. Crown 8vo. 5s.

DAINTREE. With Illustrations. Crown 8vo. 3s. 6d.

BOXALL SCHOOL. With Illustrations. Crown 8vo. 3s. 6d.

EXPELLED; or, The Story of a Young Gentleman. With Illustrations. Crown 8vo. 5s.

NISBET'S CABINET SERIES.

With Illustrations. Crown 8vo. 2s. each.

1. MATTHEW FROST, CARRIER; or, Little Snowdrop's Mission. By Mrs. MARSHALL.
2. THE SPANISH BARBER. By the Author of "Mary Powell."
3. THREE PATHS IN LIFE. A Tale for Girls. By ELLEN BARLEE.
4. STELLAFONT ABBEY; or, "Nothing New." By Mrs. MARSHALL.
5. A SUNBEAM'S INFLUENCE; or, Eight Years After. By the Hon. Mrs. CLIFFORD-BUTLER.
6. A TALE OF TWO OLD SONGS. By the Hon. Mrs. CLIFFORD-BUTLER.
7. ESTHER'S JOURNAL; or, A Tale of Swiss Pension Life. By a Resident. With a Preface by Miss WHATELY.
8. EFFIE'S FRIENDS; or, Chronicles of the Woods and Shores.
9. THERESA'S JOURNAL. From the French of Madame de Pressensé. By CRICHTON CAMPBELL.

AMERICAN TALES.

With Illustrations. Crown 8vo. 2s. 6d. each.

1. THE THREE LITTLE SPADES. By ANNA WARNER.
2. STEPPING HEAVENWARD. By Mrs. PRENTISS.
3. URBANE AND HIS FRIENDS. By Mrs. PRENTISS.
4. THE HOME AT GREYLOCK. By Mrs. PRENTISS.
5. OUR RUTH: A Story of Old Times in New England. By Mrs. PRENTISS.
6. PINE NEEDLES AND OLD YARNS. By SUSAN WARNER.
7. THE BLUE FLAG AND THE CLOTH OF GOLD. By ANNA WARNER.
8. MOTHER'S QUEER THINGS; or, A Bag of Stories. By ANNA WARNER.

"THE WORD" SERIES.

By SUSAN and ANNA WARNER, Authors of "The Wide Wide
World," "Queechy," &c.

*With Illustrations, Plain and Coloured, Handsomely bound in cloth.
Crown 8vo.   2s. 6d. each.*

The aim of this Series of Volumes is so to set forth the Bible incidents and course of history, with its train of actors, as to see them in
the circumstances and colouring, the light and shade, of their actual
existence.

The volumes embody, as far as possible, all the known facts,
natural, social, and historical, which are required for the illustration
and elucidation of the Bible narrative.

1. WALKS FROM EDEN: The Scripture Story from the Creation
   to the Death of Abraham.

   "The design of this book is excellent; most valuable and interesting
   information is communicated in a very pleasant way."—*Our Own Fireside.*

2. THE HOUSE OF ISRAEL: The Scripture Story from the Birth
   of Isaac to the Death of Jacob.

   "The amount of information conveyed, or the life and interest thrown
   into the Biblical story, would scarcely be credited by those who have not
   seen the book. . . . *This is the kind of instruction which we need for our young
   people in the present day.*"

3. THE KINGDOM OF JUDAH: The Scripture Story from the
   Death of Solomon to the Captivity.

   "We must congratulate the author on the very happy plan of the work."—
   Sunday School Chronicle.

4. THE BROKEN WALLS OF JERUSALEM AND THE RE-
   BUILDING OF THEM. In continuation of "The House of
   Israel" and "The Kingdom of Judah," and completing the
   work.

5. THE STAR OUT OF JACOB: The Scripture Story Illustrating
   the Earlier Portion of the Gospel Narrative.

   "For Sunday reading with the young, whether for the home circle or in a
   class, we are sure this work will prove a boon; and many a teacher will hail
   its advent, and find endless help in different ways."

THE GOLDEN LADDER SERIES.

With Plain and Coloured Illustrations. Crown 8vo.
3s. 6d. each.

"What need of a single word of commendation of the 'Golden Ladder Series?' Its volumes are in nearly every house in the kingdom."—*Glasgow Herald.*

1. THE GOLDEN LADDER: Stories Illustrative of the Beatitudes. By SUSAN and ANNA WARNER.
2. THE WIDE, WIDE WORLD. By SUSAN WARNER.
3. QUEECHY. By SUSAN WARNER.
4. MELBOURNE HOUSE. By SUSAN WARNER.
5. DAISY. By SUSAN WARNER.
6. DAISY IN THE FIELD. By SUSAN WARNER.
7. THE OLD HELMET. By SUSAN WARNER.
8. NETTIE'S MISSION: Stories Illustrative of the Lord's Prayer. By JULIA MATHEWS.
9. GLEN LUNA; or, Dollars and Cents. By SUSAN WARNER.
10. DRAYTON HALL. Stories Illustrative of the Beatitudes. By JULIA MATHEWS.
11. WITHIN AND WITHOUT: A New England Story.
12. VINEGAR HILL STORIES: Illustrative of the Parable of the Sower. By ANNA WARNER.
13. LITTLE SUNBEAMS. By JOANNA MATHEWS.
14. WHAT SHE COULD AND OPPORTUNITIES. By SUSAN WARNER.
15. TRADING, AND THE HOUSE IN TOWN.
16. DARE TO DO RIGHT. By JULIA MATHEWS.
17. HOLDEN WITH THE CORDS. By the Author of "Within and Without."
18. GIVING HONOUR: Containing "The Little Camp on Eagle Hill," and "Willow Brook." By SUSAN WARNER.
19. GIVING SERVICE: Containing "Sceptres and Crowns," and "The Flag of Truce." By SUSAN WARNER.
20. GIVING TRUST: Containing "Bread and Oranges," and "The Rapids of Niagara." By SUSAN WARNER.
   ** *The Tales in Vols.* 18, 19, 20 *are Illustrative of the*
   LORD'S PRAYER.
21. WYCH HAZEL. A Tale. By SUSAN and ANNA WARNER.
22. THE GOLD OF CHICKAREE. A Sequel to Wych Hazel. By SUSAN and ANNA WARNER.
23. DIANA. By SUSAN WARNER.

24. MY DESIRE. By Susan Warner.
25. THE END OF A COIL. By Susan Warner.
26. THE LETTER OF CREDIT. By Susan Warner.
27. NOBODY. By Susan Warner.
28. STEPHEN, M.D. By Susan Warner.
29. A RED WALLFLOWER. By Susan Warner.
30. BUTTERCUPS AND DAISIES. By Susan Warner.

NISBET'S ENTERTAINING LIBRARY FOR YOUNG PEOPLE.

With Illustrations. Fcap. 8vo. 1s. each.

"Pretty little books, bright in the binding, and with contents as entertaining as the exterior is attractive."—*Daily Review.*

1. GENTLEMAN JIM. By Mrs. Prentiss.
2. FRAMILODE HALL. By Mrs. Marshall.
3. A CHIP OF THE OLD BLOCK. By Mrs. Marshall.
4. THE PRINCE'S BOX; or, The Magic Mirror. By C. N. Simpson.
5. URSULA: A Story of the Bohemian Reformation.
6. OUR LADDIE. By Miss L. J. Tomlinson.
7. A VIOLET IN THE SHADE. By Mrs. Marshall.
8. LIGHT ON THE LILY. By Mrs. Marshall.
9. A ROSE WITHOUT THORNS. By Mrs. Marshall.
10. DOLLY'S CHARGE. By Miss Beatrice Marshall.
11. THE MOUNTAIN MILL. By H. C. Coape.
12. FAN'S BROTHER. By Miss Beatrice Marshall.
13. THE MAITLAND'S MONEY-BOX. By Lady Dunboyne.

NISBET'S CROWN SERIES.

With Illustrations. Crown 8vo. 1s. each.

1. THE BLACK SHEEP OF THE PARISH. By Lady Dunboyne.
2. MRS. ARNOLD. By Miss Wodehouse.
3. LET THERE BE LIGHT; or, The Story of the Reformation for Children. By Mrs. Bower.
4. SCIENCE EVENINGS WITH MY CHILDREN. By Mrs. Bower.

THE HOME AND SCHOOL SERIES.

With Illustrations. Crown. 1s. 6d.

"Very suitable for boys and girls. They are elegantly got up, and the matter, while interesting to young minds, is not without a dust of wholesome instruction."—*Glasgow Herald.*

1. AMOS FAYLE; or, Through the Wilderness into a Wealthy Place. By Mrs. PROSSER.

2. RUNNING AWAY.

3. STORIES OF THE LAND WE LIVE IN. By WILLIAM LOCKE.

4. A RAY OF LIGHT TO BRIGHTEN COTTAGE HOMES. By the Author of "A Trap to Catch a Sunbeam."

5. THE STORY OF AN OLD POCKET BIBLE, as related by Itself. By ROBERT COX, A.M.

6. ASHTON COTTAGE; or, The True Faith.

7. MARJORY. By Mrs. MARSHALL.

8. COURAGE AND COWARDS; or, Who was the Bravest? By the Author of "The Maiden of the Iceberg."

9. AGATHA LEE'S INHERITANCE. By Mrs. M. R. HIGHAM, Author of "The Other House."

10. NIDWORTH AND HIS THREE MAGIC WANDS. By Mrs. E. PRENTISS.

11. ALICE L'ESTRANGE'S MOTTO, AND HOW IT GAINED THE VICTORY. By RABY HUME.

12. FAITHFUL UNTO DEATH; or, Susine and Claude of the Val Pelice.

13. THE BIRTH OF A CENTURY; or, Eighty Years Ago. By Mrs. MARSHALL.

14. ROSE HARTLEY AND HER CHRISTMAS WAY-MARKS. By Miss REDFORD.

15. HELEN HERVEY'S CHANGE; or, Out of Darkness into Light. By MARIA ENGLISH.

16. SUMMERLAND GRANGE. By Lady DUNBOYNE.

THE SELECT SERIES OF BOOKS SUITABLE FOR PRESENTS AND PRIZES.

Small Crown 8vo. 3s. 6d. each.

1. DERRY : A Tale of the Revolution. By CHARLOTTE ELIZABETH.

2. THE FORUM AND THE VATICAN. By NEWMAN HALL, LL.B.

3. DAYS AND NIGHTS IN THE EAST; or, Illustrations of Bible Scenes. By HORATIUS BONAR, D.D.

4. THE HOLY WAR. By JOHN BUNYAN.

5. THE MOUNTAINS OF THE BIBLE : Their Scenes and their Lessons. By the Rev. JOHN MACFARLANE, LL.D.

6. LIFE : A Series of Illustrations of the Divine Wisdom in the Forms, Structures, and Instincts of Animals. By P. H. GOSSE, F.R.S.

7. LAND AND SEA. By P. H. GOSSE, F.R.S.

8. JOHN KNOX AND HIS TIMES. By the Author of "The Story of Martin Luther."

9. HOME IN THE HOLY LAND : A Tale illustrating Incidents and Customs in Modern Jerusalem. By Mrs. FINN.

10. A THIRD YEAR IN JERUSALEM : A Tale illustrating Incidents and Customs in Modern Jerusalem. By Mrs. FINN.

11 & 12. THE ROMANCE OF NATURAL HISTORY. By P. H. GOSSE, F.R.S.

13. BROOMFIELD : A Tale. By the Author of "John Knox and his Times," &c.

14. TALES FROM ALSACE ; or, Scenes and Portraits from Life in the Days of the Reformation. Translated from the German.

15. HYMNS OF THE CHURCH MILITANT. Edited by the Author of "The Wide, Wide World."

16. THE PHYSICIAN'S DAUGHTERS. By the Author of "Wandering Homes," &c.

17. WANDERING HOMES AND THER INFLUENCES. By the Author of "The Physician's Daughters."

18. BYEWAYS IN PALESTINE. By JAMES FINN, M.R.A.S.

19. THE PILGRIM'S PROGRESS. By JOHN BUNYAN. With Illustrations.

THE JUVENILE EIGHTEENPENNY SERIES.

With Illustrations. · 16mo.

"Capital books, well printed, tastefully bound, and containing a good deal of letterpress. We do not know a cheaper series at the price."—*Sunday School Chronicle.*

1. AUNT EDITH ; or, Love to God the Best Motive.
2. SUSY'S SACRIFICE. By the Author of "Nettie's Mission."
3. KENNETH FORBES ; or, Fourteen Ways of Studying the Bible.
4. LILIES OF THE VALLEY, and other Tales.
5. CLARA STANLEY ; or, A Summer among the Hills.
6. THE CHILDREN OF BLACKBERRY HOLLOW.
7. HERBERT PERCY ; or, From Christmas to Easter.
8. PASSING CLOUDS ; or, Love Conquering Evil.
9. DAYBREAK ; or, Right Struggling and Triumphant.
10. WARFARE AND WORK ; or, Life's Progress.
11. EVELYN GREY. By the Author of "Clara Stanley."
12. THE HISTORY OF THE GRAVELYN FAMILY.
13. DONALD FRASER.
14. THE SAFE COMPASS, AND HOW IT POINTS. By the Rev. R. NEWTON, D.D.
15. THE KING'S HIGHWAY ; or, Illustrations of the . Commandments. By the Rev. R. NEWTON, D.D.
16. BESSIE AT THE SEASIDE. By JOANNA H. MATHEWS.
17. CASPER. By the Author of "The Wide, Wide World."
18. KARL KRINKEN ; or, The Christmas Stocking. By the Author of "The Wide, Wide World."
19. MR. RUTHERFORD'S CHILDREN. By the Author of "The Wide, Wide World."
20. SYBIL AND CHRYSSA. By the Author of "The Wide, Wide World."
21. HARD MAPLE. By the Author of "The Wide, Wide World."
22. OUR SCHOOL DAYS.
23. AUNT MILDRED'S LEGACY.
24. MAGGIE AND BESSIE, AND THEIR WAY TO DO GOOD. By JOANNA H. MATHEWS.
25. GRACE BUXTON ; or, The Light of Home. By Mrs. MARSHALL.

THE JUVENILE EIGHTEENPENNY SERIES—continued.

26. LITTLE KATY AND JOLLY JIM. By ALICE GRAY.

27. BESSIE AT SCHOOL. By JOANNA H. MATHEWS.

28. BESSIE AND HER FRIENDS. By JOANNA H. MATHEWS.

29. BESSIE AMONG THE MOUNTAINS. By JOANNA H. MATHEWS.

30. HILDA AND HILDEBRAND; or, The Twins of Ferndale Abbey.

31. GLEN ISLA. By Mrs. DRUMMOND.

32. LUCY SEYMOUR; or, "It is more Blessed to Give than to Receive." By Mrs. DRUMMOND.

33. LOUISA MORETON; or, "Children, Obey your Parents in all Things." By Mrs. DRUMMOND.

34. THE "WILMOT FAMILY;" or, "They that Deal Truly are his Delight." By Mrs. DRUMMOND.

35. SOWING IN TEARS AND REAPING IN JOY. By FRANZ HOFFMAN. From the German, by Mrs. FABER.

36. BESSIE ON HER TRAVELS. By JOANNA H. MATHEWS.

37. LITTLE NELLIE; or, The Clockmaker's Daughter.

38. THREE LITTLE SISTERS. By Mrs. MARSHALL.

39. MABEL GRANT: A Highland Story. By RANDALL H. BALLANTYNE.

40. THE RETURN FROM INDIA. By the Author of "Hilda and Hildebrand."

41. THE COURT AND THE KILN: A Tale Founded on the Church Catechism.

42. SILVER SANDS; or, Pennie's Romance.

43. LIONEL ST. CLAIR. By the Author of "Herbert Percy."

44. THE KNOTS TOM GILLIES TIED AND UNTIED. By Mrs. G. GLADSTONE.

45. THE LITTLE PREACHER. By the Author of "Stepping Heavenward."

46. LOVE FULFILLING THE LAW.

47. ANTOINE, THE ITALIAN BOY. By the Rev. C. W. DENISON.

48. TWO LITTLE HEARTS. By SOPHIE SPICER.

49. DICK'S FIRST SCHOOL-DAYS. By Mrs. H. BARNARD.

50. THREE LITTLE BROTHERS. By Mrs. MARSHALL.

THE JUVENILE SHILLING SERIES.

With Illustrations. 16mo.

1. CHANGES UPON CHURCH BELLS. By C. S. H.
2. GONZALEZ AND HIS WAKING DREAMS. By C. S. H.
3. DAISY BRIGHT. By Mrs. MARSHALL.
4. HELEN ; or, Temper and its Consequences. By Mrs G. GLADSTONE.
5. THE CAPTAIN'S STORY ; or, The Disobedient Son. By W. S. MARTIN.
6. THE LITTLE PEAT-CUTTERS ; or, The Song of Love. By Mrs. MARSHALL.
7. LITTLE CROWNS, AND HOW TO WIN THEM. By the Rev. J. A. COLLIER.
8. CHINA AND ITS PEOPLE. By a MISSIONARY'S WIFE.
9. TEDDY'S DREAM.
10. ELDER PARK; or, Scenes in our Garden. By Mrs ALFRED PAYNE.
11. HOME LIFE AT GREYSTONE LODGE. By the Author of AGNES FALCONER.
12. THE PEMBERTON FAMILY, and other Stories.
13. CHRISTMAS AT SUNBERRY DALE. By W. B. B., Author of "Clara Downing's Dream."
14. PRIMROSE; or, The Bells of Old Effingham. By Mrs. MARSHALL.
15. THE BOY GUARDIAN. By C. E. BOWEN, Author of "Dick and his Donkey."
16. VIOLET'S IDOL. By JOANNA H. MATHEWS.
17. FRANK GORDON. By F. R. GOULDING ; and LITTLE JACK, by ANNA WARNER.
18. THE COTTAGE BY THE CREEK. By the Hon. Mrs. CLIFFORD-BUTLER.
19. THE WILD BELLS, AND WHAT THEY RANG. By W. S. MARTIN.

THE JUVENILE SHILLING SERIES—continued.

20. TO-DAY AND YESTERDAY: A Story of Summer and Winter Holidays. By Mrs. MARSHALL.
21. GLASTONBURY ; or, The Early British Christians.
22. MAX: A Story of the Oberstein Forest.
23. MARY TRELAWNY. By CHRISTIAN REDFORD.
24. LUPICINE ; or, The Hermit of St. Loup.
25. LOVING-KINDNESS ; or, The Ashdown Flower-Show.
26. BETWEEN THE CLIFFS. By Mrs. MARSHALL.
27. FRITZ ; or, The Struggles of a Young Life. By the Author of "MAX."

THE BESSIE LIBRARY,

CONTAINING

1. MAGGIE AND BESSIE.
2. BESSIE AT SCHOOL.
3. BESSIE AND HER FRIENDS.
4. BESSIE IN THE MOUNTAINS.
5. BESSIE AT THE SEASIDE.
6. BESSIE ON HER TRAVELS.

BY JOANNA H. MATHEWS.

In neat cloth box, price 10s. 6d.

LONDON:
JAMES NISBET & CO., 21 BERNERS STREET, W.

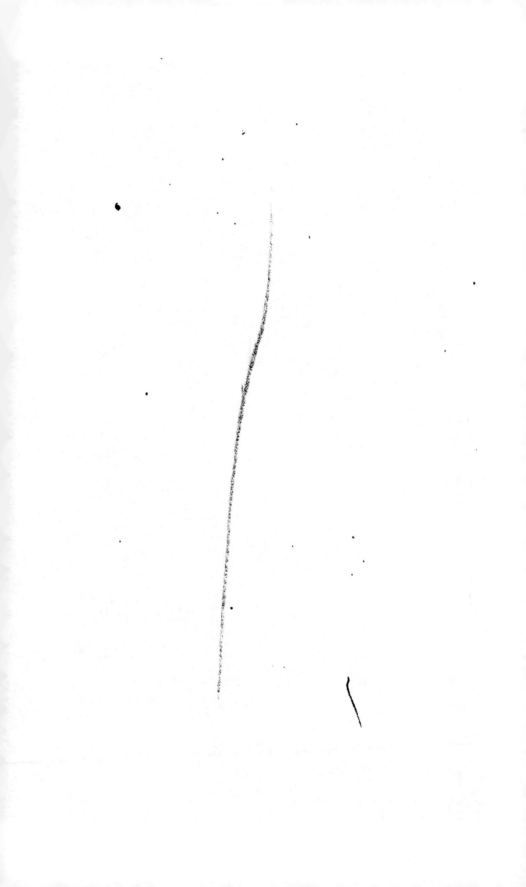